"Comprehensive and resourceful. It will become the most used cookbook in your kitchen."

—TRACEY WENDT,
owner of Good Things For All Seasons in downtown Grapevine, TX

"Momma Hensel's cooking is truly the biggest gift your taste buds will ever receive! My childhood was filled with the familiar yet phenomenal dishes from Patty's kitchen. From parties to family dinners, she was our go-to place to fill our bellies. My mouth is watering right now just thinking about her toffee. You owe it to yourself to utilize these recipes."

—CALLIE SEIFRIED,
life-time family friend

"I have known Patty Hensel for over twenty years. We started out as neighbors and have become good friends over the years. Not only is Patty a good wife and mother, she is one of the best cooks I have ever met . . . And I come from a very large extended Italian family where food is one of the main reasons for living!

Whether cooking for a school event for the kids, or dining out with our gourmet group, I always look forward to indulging in Patty's cuisine. It doesn't get much better than when Patty calls us up after their family has just finished dinner, and asks us if we would like to have some of the 'extra' food that she has prepared.

My favorite dishes are her Lasagna and anything Tex-Mex. But her piéce de résistance is her home-made "crab chowder!" It is absolutely the best that I have ever tasted anywhere . . . hands down!

So, I want to wish Patty a well-deserved congratulations on the publishing of new her cookbook. Her sharing of her delicious recipes with everyone else is long overdue.

Buon Appetito!"

—LARRY COMPO,
long-time friend and neighbor
Colleyville, TX

"One wonderful book with all the recipes a girl needs from her 'Momma Hensel' to start her home as a woman. Every girl needs this book in her kitchen!"

—YASMEEN KHEDERY,
life-time family friend

Momma's Treasures

Wishing you years of delicious home cooked meals to help make your kitchen the heart of the home.
♡ Happy Cooking!
Patty Hensel

Follow me on Instagram:
@mommastreasures

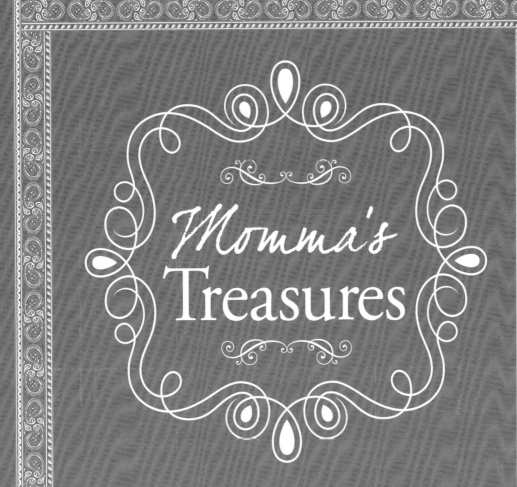

Momma's Treasures

The Only Cookbook You Will Need to
Make Your Own Collection of Family Favorites

Patty Hensel

BROWN BOOKS
PUBLISHING GROUP

© 2015 Patty Hensel

All rights reserved. No part of this book may be used or reproduced in any manner without written permission except in the case of brief quotations embodied in critical articles or reviews.

Momma's Treasures

Brown Books Publishing Group
16250 Knoll Trail Drive, Suite 205
Dallas, Texas 75248
www.BrownBooks.com
(972) 381-0009

A New Era in Publishing™

ISBN 978-1-61254-174-7
LCCN 2015930824

Printed in the United States
10 9 8 7 6 5 4 3 2 1

For more information or to contact the author, please go to
www.MommasTreasuresBook.com
www.PattyHensel.com

To Steve, my soul mate for over thirty years, through thick and thin, from twenty to fifty-five years old, from a garage apartment to our home for twenty-five years, from medical school to oh-so-close retirement. You will always be my own personal doctor. God only knows where I'd be without you.

To my two beautiful daughters Amber and Lauren. I still remember when I first found out I was pregnant and worrying that I would not know how to be a mom, and then pregnant again wondering how I could love another. I have cherished every moment being your mom.

To Tricia, my first best friend whom we lost way too soon. Hardly a day goes by that I do not think of you. You were my roommate, my maid-of-honor, and my best friend; our relationship lasted over two decades. My only regret in life is that you are not here with me, growing old together. I realized way too late how important a lifelong best friend is. I know you are at peace and watching over your precious family. How awesome they have become; you must be beaming looking down.

To all of my friends and family whom I have cooked for the past 30 years. I was blessed with a large extended family, and I am always looking forward to the next event.

To all of the young ladies I have watched grow from little girls with pigtails to awesome beautiful women inside and out. May all of you become amazing cooks yourselves. The heart of the home starts in the kitchen.

Contents

ACKNOWLEDGMENTS	x
FROM MY KITCHEN TO YOURS	xi
BASIC EQUIPMENT FOR A BEGINNING COOK: MUST-HAVES ON A WEDDING REGISTRY	xiii
MEASUREMENTS AND EQUIVALENTS	xiv
BEVERAGES	1
BRUNCH	9
DIPS	27
APPETIZERS/SNACKS	41
SOUPS	57
SALADS	71
DRESSINGS, MARINADES, AND SAUCES	89

BREADS	109
SIDE DISHES	117
PASTA AND RICE	139
MAIN DISHES	
BEEF	147
POULTRY	167
SEAFOOD	199
PORK	217
DESSERTS	
COOKIES	229
CAKES	243
PIES	265
OTHERS	273
INDEX	289
ABOUT THE AUTHOR	313

Acknowledgments

I would like to thank my family for their patience when I was ignoring them.

I would like to thank Tracey, Larry, Callie, and Yasmeen for their endorsements.

I would like to thank Janet Harris and Kathy Penny from Brown Books. Without their confidence in my cookbook, I doubt it would have materialized.

Finally, I would like thank God. "I can do all things through Christ who strengthens me"—Philippians 4:13

I may not be there yet, but I'm closer than I was yesterday—Unknown Author

I'm not anything until I'm everything.

From My Kitchen to Yours

I come from a long line of amazing cooks. Not chefs but cooks. There is a difference in my family.

My heritage is German. My maternal grandmother, Paula Weiderstein, came from Germany with her three sisters: Metta, Nealey, and Olga. She married Albert Kattner, a Methodist minister, and they lived in New Braunfels, Texas, where I was born in 1961. I called them "Momo" and "Popo."

My daddy's mom, Grandma Lane, had "supper" ready at the same time every day. She and Grandpa Emmett lived in a small East Texas town called Tenaha, which has a population of about one thousand. The home they lived in until they could no longer had electricity but no phone or running water. I still remember my grandma carrying water from the well and using the "outhouse." Grandma Lane was also the cook for the town's school cafeteria, something she loved to do to the delight of all the school children from kindergarten through senior year.

All of our family gatherings revolved around food: church socials, picnics, birthday parties, reunions, and so on. I remember watching Momo, Grandma Lane, my mom, and aunts cooking without recipes, remembering details by the hundreds. Back then I was amazed, but now I find myself doing the same thing.

With my awesome husband, Steve, whom I married in 1982, I am the proud mother of two beautiful and amazing daughters, Amber and Lauren. When my oldest began asking me to show her how to cook, I realized I'm not a good teacher. Instead I decided to compile some recipes for her to use. This project ended with more than three hundred handwritten recipe cards, dog-eared family cookbook pages, and some copies of Momo's recipes. Many were stuffed into an old recipe box that I started when

I first got married. Finding a specific recipe when I wanted it was almost impossible. That led me to write this cookbook. Now recipes are organized and much easier to find and to follow.

I also realized the book needed a title. A few years back, I got the nickname "Momma Hensel" after years of event planning for my daughters and their friends, volunteering as event photographer, serving on the PTA board, and acting as crossing guard at our local elementary school. I cherish it as a name of endearment; it inspired the title of this collection of treasured family recipes selected from the hundreds I've compiled. These recipes are my favorites; most are quick and easy to make. I have written detailed directions, so recipes are easy to follow. I hope some of these recipes become your favorites too.

Basic Equipment for a Beginning Cook: Must-Haves on a Wedding Registry

- Set of glass mixing bowls
- Set of plastic mixing bowls with pouring spouts
- Set of measuring cups
- Large (2- or 4-cup) measuring cup
- Measuring spoons
- Set of knives, including paring and serrated bread knives
- Kitchen shears
- Hand chopper
- Large and small bowl food processors
- Utensils, including spatula, slotted spoon, and pasta fork
- Soup ladle
- Pie and cake servers
- Tongs
- Whisk
- Garlic press
- Vegetable peeler
- Pastry brush
- Potato masher
- Rolling pin
- Wooden spoons
- Handheld grater
- Large and small cutting boards
- Colander
- Fine mesh strainer
- Potholders
- Apron
- Ice bucket
- Bottle opener
- Wine opener
- Salt and pepper grinders
- Storage containers
- Handheld mixer
- 10- or 12-piece set of pots and pans
- Glass or porcelain bake ware, including 9″ x 13″ pan, 9″ square pan, and loaf pan
- Metal ovenware, including cookie sheet, 9″ x 13″ pan, 9″ x 5″ pan, two 8″ round cake pans, and muffin and mini-muffin pans
- Two wire racks for cooling
- Pizza stone
- Slow cooker such as the Ninja All-in-One Cooking System
- Panini press
- Waffle iron
- Coffee maker
- Toaster
- Can opener
- Blender

Measurements and Equivalents

Teaspoons and Tablespoons	Equivalent
Under 1/8 teaspoon	Dash
3 teaspoons	1 tablespoons
4 tablespoons	1/4 cup = 2 ounces
5 1/3 tablespoons	1/3 cup
8 tablespoons	1/2 cup = 4 ounces
10 2/3 tablespoons	2/3 cup
12 tablespoons	3/4 cup = 6 ounces
16 tablespoons	1 cup = 8 ounces

Cups	Equivalent
1/8 cup	1 ounce = 2 tablespoons
1/4 cup	2 ounces = 4 tablespoons
1/3 cup	2.6 ounces = 5 tablespoons plus 1 teaspoon
1/2 cup	4 ounces = 8 tablespoons
3/4 cup	6 ounces = 12 tablespoons
1 cup	8 ounces = 16 tablespoons
2 cups	16 ounces = 1 pint
4 cups	1 quart
8 cups	2 quarts = 1/2 gallon
16 cups	4 quarts = 1 gallon

Beverages

TIP

Frozen grapes can be used to chill
wine without watering it down.

Instant Hot Chocolate

Makes 3 quarts

1 30-ounce package Nestlé Nesquik chocolate flavor powder

1 8-quart box instant confectioners' milk

1 16-ounce box powdered sugar

1 6-ounce container Coffee-Mate

Combine all ingredients in a large bowl; mix well.

To serve, stir 1/3 cup mix into 1 cup (8 ounces) of hot water until dissolved.

For homemade Christmas gifts, place pint or quart portions of the mix into decorated tins or Mason jars.

Dry Mix Spiced Tea

Makes 3 quarts

2 cups Tang drink mix

1 cup instant tea

2 cups sugar

2 2-quart packages sweetened lemonade mix

1 tablespoon cinnamon

1 teaspoon cloves

1 teaspoon nutmeg

Combine all ingredients in a large bowl or container, mixing well. Store in airtight containers or jars.

To serve, stir 1 tablespoon mix into 8 ounces of boiling water until dissolved.

Bahama Rum Punch

Makes 5 to 6 servings

1 cup Bacardi gold rum

1 cup coconut rum

2 cups pineapple juice

2 cups orange juice

1/4 cup grenadine bar syrup

Combine ingredients in large pitcher or bowl; chill.

To serve, pour over ice in glasses. Garnish each glass with a maraschino cherry and a slice of fresh orange.

Summer Wine Cooler

Makes 6 to 8 servings

1 750ml bottle white wine

2 12-ounce cans Sprite or 7 Up

Juice from 1 orange

Juice from 1 lemon

Juice from 1 lime

Lime slices for garnish

In large pitcher, combine all ingredients except the lime slices and chill.

To serve, pour over ice (or frozen grapes) in glasses. Garnish with the lime slices.

Sangria

Makes 6 to 8 servings

1 lemon, sliced thin
1 orange, sliced thin
1 lime, sliced thin
3/4 cup gin
1 750ml bottle Cabernet Sauvignon or other dry red wine
1/2 cup orange juice
1/4 cup cranberry juice
1/2 cup tonic water

Layer the lemon, lime, and orange slices in the bottom of a large pitcher. Pour gin over the fruit; cover and refrigerate overnight. Just before serving, add the remaining ingredients and stir; chill.

To serve, pour over ice into glasses.

Hot Buttered Rum

Makes 4 servings

4 tablespoons butter, at room temperature
2 tablespoons dark brown sugar
4 teaspoons pumpkin pie spice
4 ounces dark rum
2 cups apple cider, heated until almost boiling

In a small bowl, using a whisk or spoon, mix together softened butter, brown sugar, and pie spice until smooth; chill until firm.

To serve, divide butter mixture among four mugs. Pour 1/2 cup hot cider and 1 ounce dark rum into each.

KATTNER STRAWBERRY JELL-O JUICE PUNCH

Makes 2 gallons, approximately 32 4-ounce servings

1 quart water
2 3-ounce packages Strawberry Jell-O
1 46-ounce can pineapple juice
1 6-ounce can frozen lemonade concentrate
2 cups sugar
Additional water to make 2 gallons

Place water in saucepan and bring to a boil. Add Jell-O, stirring to dissolve. Lower heat and simmer 3 minutes.

In 2-gallon container, combine Jell-O, pineapple juice, lemonade, sugar, and enough water to make 2 gallons. Stir well and chill for several hours until very cold.

To serve, place in large punch bowl with a large chunk of ice, if desired. Ladle into punch cups.

EASY SHOWER PUNCH

Makes 48 servings

1/2 gallon lime or orange sherbet
1 32-ounce bottle ginger ale, chilled
2 32-ounce bottles Sprite or 7 Up, chilled

Scoop sherbet into a large punch bowl. Pour the ginger ale and Sprite or 7 Up over the sherbet, mixing gently.

To serve, ladle liquid into punch cups, adding a dollop of sherbet in each.

Pink Elephant Punch

Makes 48 servings

2 quarts cranberry juice
2 cups pineapple juice
1 quart ginger ale
1 1-liter bottle vodka

Chill all ingredients.

Pour water into ring mold or Bundt pan and freeze solid. If desired, arrange grape bunches in water before freezing to make a pretty garnish.

Combine chilled ingredients in large pitcher and mix to combine.

To serve, place ice ring in large punch bowl. Pour chilled punch into bowl over ice ring. Ladle into punch cups.

This potent concoction makes a pretty shower punch.

Brunch

TIP

Only green hydrangeas can be dried and used as decorations. Hang the stems upside down on the clips of a pant hanger and leave hanging for a couple of days.

French Toast

Makes 5 servings

5 eggs
1 cup milk
1/2 teaspoon salt
1/2 teaspoon fresh ground pepper
2 tablespoons butter
10 slices thin sandwich bread
1 tablespoon powdered sugar
Maple syrup, as desired

In a medium bowl, whisk together the eggs, milk, salt, and pepper.

Heat griddle to 350 degrees. When griddle is hot, add butter and swirl to cover the surface. Dip each slice of bread into the egg mixture to coat both sides. Place on heated griddle. Cook for about 8 to 10 minutes, turning once, until brown on both sides.

Sprinkle slices with powdered sugar. Serve with syrup.

Homestyle Waffles

Makes 6 to 8 waffles

3 eggs
1 cup milk
1/2 cup butter, melted
1 tablespoon vanilla
2 cups flour
1/2 teaspoon salt
1 tablespoon baking powder
1 teaspoon sugar

Break eggs into a medium bowl. Using a whisk or handheld electric mixer, beat eggs until thick and light yellow in color. Mix in milk, butter, and vanilla.

Combine dry ingredients in medium bowl, stirring to combine. Fold dry ingredients into egg mixture and mix well.

Preheat waffle iron. Following manufacturer's instructions, bake batter to make waffles.

Breakfast Bacon Burritos

Makes 6 burritos

12 slices bacon

1 cup refrigerated hash browns potatoes

2 tablespoons butter

4 eggs

1/2 cup milk

1 teaspoon salt

1/2 teaspoon fresh ground pepper

10 tablespoons salsa, divided

1/2 cup shredded Cheddar cheese, optional

1/4 cup sour cream, optional

6 large flour tortillas

In a large skillet over medium-high heat, arrange bacon in single layer and cook until crisp. Remove and drain on paper towels. Pour off all but about one tablespoon bacon drippings. Place hash browns in pan with the drippings and cook until brown and crisp; remove and drain on paper towels.

Add the butter to the skillet and melt. In a medium bowl, mix the eggs, milk, salt, and pepper with a whisk. Pour egg mixture into the heated skillet and cook for 2 to 4 minutes, stirring frequently. Remove from heat and stir in 4 tablespoons of salsa.

In each tortilla, place 2 tablespoons of the eggs, 2 slices of bacon, 2 to 3 tablespoons of the hash browns, and cheese, as desired. Roll and wrap in paper towels. Continue for each tortilla.

When ready to serve, microwave for 15 to 20 seconds to heat through. Serve with additional salsa and sour cream.

Sausage Brunch Casserole

Makes 6 to 8 servings

1 pound bulk breakfast sausage, regular or spicy

1 8-ounce can crescent rolls

1 cup shredded Monterey Jack cheese

4 eggs, beaten

3/4 cup milk

1/2 teaspoon salt

1/4 teaspoon fresh ground pepper

Grease a 9″ x 13″ baking dish. Preheat oven to 375 degrees.

Crumble sausage in a medium skillet; cook until brown; drain on paper towels.

Line the bottom of greased baking dish with the crescent rolls, pressing perforations to seal. Sprinkle with the sausage and cheese.

Combine eggs, milk, salt, and pepper in a medium bowl, mixing well. Pour over sausage.

Bake until firm, approximately 20 to 25 minutes. Remove from oven and let stand 5 minutes; cut into squares.

This dish may be made the night before.
It is a Hensel family tradition for Christmas.

Tortilla Morning

Makes 12 to 15 servings

1 pound bulk pork breakfast sausage

10 corn tortillas, cut into quarters

12 eggs

1/2 cup milk

1 teaspoon salt

1/2 teaspoon fresh ground pepper

1 11- to 15-ounce can Mexicorn, drained

1 cup shredded Cheddar cheese

1 1/2 cups salsa

1 cup sour cream

1 cup guacamole

Crumble and brown the sausage in a medium skillet over medium-high heat; drain on paper towels.

Arrange tortilla pieces evenly over the bottom of a greased 9″ x 13″ baking dish. Sprinkle sausage over the tortillas.

In a medium bowl, whisk the eggs, milk, salt, and pepper until blended. Stir in the corn. Pour the egg mixture over the tortillas. Sprinkle with the cheese. Cover tightly with foil and refrigerate for 8 to 10 hours.

Bake, covered with foil, in a preheated 375-degree oven for 25 to 30 minutes or just until the eggs are firm. Turn off oven and remove dish from oven.

Discard foil. Spread top of casserole with the salsa and place back in the oven, uncovered, for 5 to 10 minutes to meld. Remove from oven and let set for 5 minutes.

Serve with the sour cream and guacamole as garnish.

Easy Brunch Casserole

Makes 4 to 6 servings

8 slices bacon

2 cups croutons, plain or seasoned

1 cup shredded Cheddar cheese

4 eggs, beaten

2 cups milk

1/2 teaspoon salt

1/4 teaspoon fresh ground pepper

1/2 teaspoon prepared mustard

1/2 teaspoon onion powder

Grease bottom of a 9" x 13" baking dish. Preheat oven to 325 degrees.

In a large skillet over medium-high heat, cook the bacon until crisp. Crumble bacon and set aside.

Layer croutons in bottom of greased baking dish. Sprinkle with cheese.

In a medium bowl, combine eggs, milk, salt, pepper, mustard, and onion powder. Mix until well-blended. Pour over cheese in baking dish. Sprinkle with bacon bits.

Bake for 55 to 60 minutes or until eggs are firm. Remove from oven and let stand for 5 minutes.

Southwest Egg Casserole

Makes 8 to 10 servings

1 pound bulk pork breakfast sausage

2 cups refrigerated hash brown potatoes

12 eggs

2 cups milk

1 teaspoon salt

1/2 teaspoon fresh ground pepper

1 teaspoon dry mustard

1/4 cup green chilies, drained

1 cup shredded Cheddar cheese

Grease a 9″ x 13″ baking dish. Preheat oven to 350 degrees.

In a medium skillet, crumble and fry the sausage until brown and cooked through; drain on paper towels. Drain the sausage drippings, leaving about 1 tablespoon in the skillet. Cook hash browns in drippings until crisp; drain on paper towels and set aside.

In a medium bowl, whisk the eggs, milk, salt, pepper, and dry mustard until blended. Stir in the green chilies. Layer the hash brown potatoes, sausage, and cheese in greased baking pan. Pour the egg mixture over layers of potatoes, sausage, and cheese.

Bake for 45 to 60 minutes or until top is firm.

Easy Breakfast Casserole

Makes about 6 servings

3 cups refrigerated hash brown potatoes

3/4 cup shredded Colby Jack cheese

1 cup ham, cut into small bite-size cubes

1/4 cup finely chopped onion

1/4 cup finely chopped green bell pepper

4 large eggs, beaten

1 1/2 cups whole milk

1/2 teaspoon salt

1/2 teaspoon fresh ground pepper

Coat a 2-quart baking dish with cooking spray. Spread the hash browns evenly in the bottom of the dish and top with the cheese, ham, onions, and bell peppers.

In a separate bowl, whisk together the eggs, milk, salt, and pepper. Pour mixture over ingredients in baking dish. Cover tightly and refrigerate overnight.

Remove casserole from the refrigerator and let stand at room temperature while oven preheats to 350 degrees. Bake uncovered for about 45 minutes or until a knife inserted in the middle comes out clean. Let stand for 5 minutes before serving.

This dish must be made a day ahead.

Southwest Ham and Potato Chip Skillet
Makes 6 servings

12 large eggs
1 5-ounce bag jalapeño potato chips, lightly crushed
1/4 cup extra-virgin olive oil
1 pound ham steak, cut into bite-size cubes
3 large green onions, sliced and finely chopped
1 teaspoon salt
1/2 teaspoon fresh ground pepper

Preheat the broiler and position a rack 8 inches from the heat.

In a large bowl, beat eggs with salt and pepper until fluffy. Add the potato chips and mash to break them up.

In a large ovenproof, non-stick skillet, heat the olive oil over medium heat. Add the diced ham and onions; cook over medium heat for 4 to 5 minutes or until lightly browned. Add the eggs and cook until set in the bottom and sides, about 3 to 4 minutes.

Place skillet in the preheated oven under broiler for about 2 minutes or until the top is lightly browned and eggs are set. Remove from oven.

Slide onto a plate and cut into wedges to serve.

This breakfast favorite is really easy to make.

Basic Ham and Cheese Quiche

Makes 4 to 6 servings

1 9" refrigerated pie crust

2 tablespoons olive oil

1 tablespoon butter

2 tablespoons finely chopped yellow onion

1/2 cup finely chopped fresh flat-leaf parsley

4 large eggs

3/4 cup half-and-half

1 cup grated Gruyère cheese

1 cup lean ham, chopped in small bite-size pieces

1 teaspoon salt

1/2 teaspoon fresh ground pepper

Preheat oven to 375 degrees. Line a pie pan with crust and set aside.

Heat the oil and the butter in a large skillet over medium-low heat. Sauté the onion until soft, about 5 to 7 minutes. Stir in the parsley.

In a large bowl, whisk together the eggs and half-and-half. Stir in onion mixture, cheese, and ham. Season with salt and pepper, mixing well.

Pour egg mixture into the pie crust. Bake until a knife inserted in the middle comes out clean, about 35 to 40 minutes. Let stand for 5 minutes.

Spinach Quiche

Makes 4 to 6 servings

1 9" refrigerated pie crust

8 slices bacon

2 cups shredded Monterey Jack cheese

1 10-ounce package frozen chopped spinach, thawed and drained

1 1/2 cups milk

3 eggs, beaten

1/2 teaspoon salt

1/2 teaspoon fresh ground pepper

1 tablespoon flour

Preheat oven to 350 degrees. Line a pie plate with crust and set aside.

In a large skillet, cook the bacon until crisp. Drain on paper towels and crumble. Sprinkle half of the crumbled bacon over bottom of pie crust.

In a medium bowl, mix together the cheese, spinach, milk, eggs, salt, pepper, and flour. Pour into the pie crust. Sprinkle remaining bacon on top.

Bake for 60 minutes or until center is firm.

Quick Cheese Puffs

Makes 40 to 48 pieces

1 can homestyle (not flaky) refrigerated biscuits

1/4 cup grated Parmesan cheese

1/4 cup grated Cheddar cheese

4 tablespoons butter, melted

Preheat oven to 425 degrees. Spray a cookie sheet with cooking spray.

Separate the biscuits and cut each into quarters.

In a small bowl, mix the cheeses together. Roll each quarter biscuit in the melted butter and then in the grated cheeses.

Place biscuit pieces on prepared cookie sheet 1/2 inch apart. Bake for 15 minutes. Serve warm.

Sausage and Egg Muffins

Makes 22 muffins

16 ounces bulk pork breakfast sausage

1/2 cup finely chopped green onions

12 eggs, beaten

2 cups shredded Cheddar cheese

1 teaspoon garlic powder

1/2 teaspoon salt

1/2 teaspoon fresh ground pepper

Preheat oven to 350 degrees.

In medium skillet, brown sausage and onion over medium heat; drain on paper towels.

In a large bowl, combine the eggs, cheese, garlic powder, salt, and pepper, mixing well. Add the sausage mixture and mix well again.

Spoon into greased muffin pans, filling 2/3 full. Bake for 25 minutes or until a pick comes out clean.

SAUSAGE BALLS

Makes 36 to 40 pieces

16 ounces bulk pork breakfast sausage
16 ounces shredded Cheddar cheese
2 cups Bisquick

Preheat oven to 350 degrees.

Mix all ingredients together until sausage, cheese, and Bisquick are evenly distributed. Mixture will be stiff.

Drop by teaspoonfuls onto an ungreased cookie sheet. Cook for 10 to 15 minutes or until golden. Serve warm or cold.

This is an all-time party favorite.

FRENCH BREAKFAST PUFFS

Makes 24 to 32 mini-muffins

2 cups Bisquick
3/4 cup butter, melted, divided use
1 cup sugar, divided
1 egg, slightly beaten
2/3 cup milk
1 tablespoon cinnamon

Preheat oven to 350 degrees. Grease bottom and sides of mini-muffin pans.

In a medium bowl, mix together the Bisquick, 1/4 cup of the melted butter, 1/2 cup sugar, egg, and milk until smooth.

Spoon into prepared mini-muffin pans, filling 2/3 full. Bake for 15 minutes.

Meanwhile, combine remaining 1/2 cup sugar and cinnamon, mixing well.

When the mini-muffins are cool enough to touch, dip each in the remaining melted butter and then into cinnamon/sugar mixture.

Cinnamon-Swirl Sour Cream Coffee Cake Muffins
Makes 18 muffins

1/2 cup packed dark brown sugar
1/4 cup finely chopped pecans
2 teaspoons cinnamon
1 cup sugar
1/4 cup butter, softened at room temperature
2 eggs, beaten
1 cup sour cream
2 tablespoons water
1 teaspoon vanilla
1 3/4 cups flour
1 teaspoon baking powder
1/2 teaspoon baking soda
1/2 teaspoon salt
6 tablespoons powdered sugar
1 tablespoon fresh orange juice
Dash salt

Preheat oven to 400 degrees.

Combine dark brown sugar, pecans, and cinnamon and set aside.

In a large bowl, beat the sugar and butter at medium speed until well-blended, about 3 minutes. Add eggs and beat another 3 minutes. Beat in the sour cream, water, and vanilla.

Combine the flour, baking powder, baking soda, and salt in another bowl, stirring well. Make a well in the center of the dry ingredients and add the sour cream mixture. Stir until just combined.

Place 3 tablespoons brown sugar mixture in a small bowl and set aside. Sprinkle surface of muffin batter with remaining brown sugar mixture. Gently fold batter four times.

Spray muffin pans with cooking spray. Spoon batter into prepared cups, filling 2/3 full. Sprinkle batter of each muffin evenly with reserved brown sugar mixture. Bake for 25 minutes or until pick inserted comes out clean. Remove and cool on wire rack.

Combine powdered sugar, juice, and a dash of salt in a small bowl, stirring until smooth. Drizzle over muffins.

Cinnamon Coffee Cakes
Makes 12 servings

2 cups flour

1 1/2 cups sugar

2 teaspoons cinnamon

1/2 teaspoon salt

1/2 cup butter, cut into pieces, chilled

1 cup finely chopped pecans

1 egg, beaten

1 cup buttermilk

1 teaspoon baking soda

Preheat oven to 350 degrees. Grease two 8″ round cake pans.

Combine the flour, sugar, cinnamon, and salt in a medium bowl and mix well. Using two knives or a pastry blender, cut in the butter until flour is crumbly. Stir in the pecans. Set aside 1/2 cup of this pecan crumb mixture.

Combine the remaining crumb mixture with the egg and mix well. Combine the buttermilk and baking soda in a small bowl and mix well. Add to the egg mixture and mix well.

Spoon the batter into greased baking pans. Sprinkle with the reserved crumb mixture.

Bake for 25 to 30 minutes or until a pick inserted in top of cake comes out clean.

These coffee cakes may be baked in disposable aluminum cake pans and frozen, covered, for future use. Thaw at room temperature or in refrigerator 8 to 10 hours.

Brunch Potatoes

Makes 6 to 8 servings

2 tablespoons butter

2 tablespoons olive oil

1/2 large red onion, sliced 1/2" thick

3 cloves garlic, finely chopped

1 teaspoon salt

1 teaspoon Cavender's All-Purpose Greek Seasoning

1 teaspoon fresh ground pepper

6 Yukon Gold potatoes, peeled, halved, and cut into bite-size pieces

In a medium skillet, heat the butter and olive oil over medium-high heat. Add onions, garlic, and spices. Sauté for 2 minutes. Add potatoes and cook uncovered for 10 to 15 minutes or until potatoes are brown and tender, stirring often.

Southwest Hash Browns

Makes 6 to 8 servings

8 ounces Mexican chorizo sausage, casings removed

1/3 cup finely chopped onion

1/2 cup finely chopped red or yellow sweet pepper

3 cloves garlic, finely chopped

1/2 teaspoon ground cumin

1 teaspoon salt

1 teaspoon Cavender's All-Purpose Greek Seasoning

1/2 teaspoon fresh ground pepper

6 Yukon Gold potatoes, peeled, halved, and cut into bite-size pieces

In a large skillet, cook the chorizo over medium-high heat until cooked through, breaking into pieces with a spoon. Remove chorizo and drain on paper towels.

Reserve 1 tablespoon of the chorizo drippings in the skillet. Add the onions, peppers, garlic, cumin, salt, pepper, and Cavender's; cook for 2 to 3 minutes. Add the potatoes and cook for 10 to 15 minutes or until potatoes are golden brown and vegetables are tender, stirring frequently. Add chorizo, stir to combine, and heat through.

Dips

TIP

Deli/rotisserie chicken can be used for recipes calling for cooked chicken.

Spinach Dip

Makes 10 to 12 servings

1 cup sour cream
1 cup mayonnaise
1 1.4-ounce package Knorr Vegetable Recipe (soup) Mix
1 10-ounce package frozen chopped spinach, thawed, drained, and squeezed
1 8-ounce can water chestnuts, finely chopped
3 green onions, sliced and finely chopped
1 loaf Hawaiian sweet round bread

Combine all ingredients except bread loaf, mixing until well-combined. Place in container with tight-fitting lid and refrigerate overnight.

To serve, cut off the top of the loaf and hollow out the middle of the Hawaiian sweet bread loaf to form a "bread bowl." Make sure external crust is thick and sturdy enough to hold the dip. Cut the inside of the loaf into bite-size pieces and serve with the dip.

Spoon the dip into the cut out area when ready to serve.

Hot Artichoke Dip

Makes 6 to 8 servings

1 8-ounce can artichoke hearts, drained and finely chopped
1 cup grated Parmesan cheese
1 cup mayonnaise
2 tablespoons finely chopped green onions, tops only
1/2 teaspoon garlic powder
1/4 teaspoon paprika

Preheat oven to 350 degrees. Coat bottom and sides of a small baking dish with cooking spray.

In a medium bowl, combine all ingredients except paprika, mixing well. Pour into prepared baking dish. Sprinkle with the paprika.

Bake for 20 to 30 minutes or until bubbly and lightly browned on top.

Serve warm with French bread, crackers, or vegetables sticks.

Virginia Hot Crab Dip

Makes 6 to 8 servings

1 8-ounce package cream cheese, softened at room temperature

1/2 cup sour cream

2 tablespoons mayonnaise

1 tablespoon lemon juice

1 teaspoon Worcestershire sauce

1/2 teaspoon dry mustard

1 teaspoon Tabasco sauce

1 tablespoon milk

3 tablespoons dry white wine

1 clove garlic, finely chopped

2 tablespoons finely chopped green onions

6 ounces fresh lump crabmeat

1/2 cup grated Parmesan cheese, divided use

Preheat oven to 350 degrees. Coat 1-quart baking dish with cooking spray.

In a medium bowl, mix all of the ingredients except cheese. Stir in 1/4 cup Parmesan cheese, reserving remainder. Pour into prepared baking dish and top with remaining cheese.

Bake for 25 to 30 minutes or until bubbly and lightly browned.

Serve warm with French bread, crackers, or vegetables sticks.

Guacamole

Makes 6 to 8 servings

2 medium avocados, peeled and seeds removed (reserve 1 avocado seed)

2 tablespoons finely chopped red onion

1 tomato, peeled, seeded, and chopped

1 tablespoon Worcestershire sauce

2 tablespoons lime juice

1 tablespoon bottled picante sauce

2 cloves garlic, finely chopped

2 tablespoons finely chopped fresh cilantro

1 teaspoon salt

1 teaspoon finely chopped, seeded fresh jalapeño pepper (optional or to taste)

Place avocados in a small bowl and mash with a potato masher. Add remaining ingredients and mix well. Push reserved avocado seed in middle of dip; cover tightly with plastic wrap to seal out air. This helps prevent browning. Refrigerate up to 2 hours to blend flavors.

Serve with tortilla or other corn chips.

Southwest Avocado and Corn Dip
Makes 10 to 12 servings

4 large avocados, peeled, seeded, and chopped
1 large tomato, peeled, seeded, and chopped
2 tablespoons finely chopped red onion
3 green onions, sliced very thin
1 11- to 15-ounce can Mexicorn, drained
1 16-ounce can black beans, drained and rinsed
1/2 cup red wine vinegar
1/2 cup vegetable oil
1 0.7-ounce package Good Seasons Italian Dressing and Recipe Mix
1 0.7-ounce package Good Seasons Zesty Italian Dressing and Recipe Mix

Toss together fresh and canned ingredients in a large bowl.

In a jar with a lid, combine vinegar, oil, and contents of dressing packets. Tighten lid and shake vigorously to combine.

Pour over vegetables and toss gently to coat vegetables. Cover and refrigerate 4 to 6 hours to blend flavors.

Serve with corn tortilla chips.

Mexican Layer Dip

Makes 6 to 8 servings

2 tablespoons olive oil

2 tablespoons finely chopped onion

1 teaspoon garlic salt

1 pound lean ground beef

3 tablespoons taco seasoning

1 16-ounce jar picante sauce

1 9-ounce can bean dip

1 8-ounce container avocado dip or 1 cup guacamole (see page 31)

1 8-ounce package grated Cheddar cheese

1 8-ounce carton or 1 cup sour cream

2 tablespoons tomatoes, peeled, seeded, and chopped

1 tablespoon finely chopped green onions

1 3.8-ounce can sliced black olives

Heat a medium skillet over medium-high heat. Add oil. When oil is hot, stir in onions and garlic salt; cook for 2 minutes. Add the meat and cook until brown. Stir in taco seasoning to coat meat and onions. Cool slightly.

In a glass casserole dish, layer ingredients in this order: meat and onion mixture, picante sauce, bean dip, avocado dip, grated cheese, and sour cream. Top with tomatoes, onions, and black olives.

Serve immediately with tortilla or favorite corn chips.

Texas Trash Warm Bean Dip

Makes 6 to 8 servings

1 8-ounce package cream cheese, softened at room temperature

1 8-ounce carton or 1 cup sour cream

2 16-ounce cans refried beans

1 1.25-ounce package taco seasoning mix

2 cups shredded Cheddar cheese

2 cups shredded Monterey Jack cheese

Preheat oven to 350 degrees. Coat a 9" x 13" baking dish with cooking spray.

In a large bowl, combine cream cheese and sour cream. Blend in refried beans until evenly blended. Stir in taco seasoning.

Spread mixture evenly into the bottom of the prepared baking dish. Sprinkle the top with cheeses. Bake for 25 to 30 minutes or until cheese is melted and slightly browned.

Serve with tortilla chips or corn chips.

Pico de Gallo

Makes 6 to 8 servings

2 large tomatoes, peeled, seeded, and finely chopped

1 jalapeño, seeded and finely chopped

1/4 cup finely chopped red onion

1 tablespoon finely chopped fresh cilantro

1 tablespoon fresh lime juice

In a small bowl, combine all ingredients; cover tightly, and chill to blend flavors.

Serve with tortilla chips or corn chips.

Chili Cheese Dip

Makes 6 to 8 servings

1 tablespoon vegetable oil
1 pound lean ground beef
2 tablespoons finely chopped onion
1/2 teaspoon garlic salt
1/2 teaspoon chili powder
1 10-ounce can Rotel diced tomatoes and green chilies
1 10-ounce can all-meat chili
8 ounces Velveeta cheese, cut into cubes

In a medium skillet, heat the oil over medium-high heat. Add the meat, onion, and garlic salt; cook until meat is no longer pink. Pour off any grease.

In a medium microwave-safe bowl, combine meat mixture with chili powder, tomatoes and green chilies, chili, and cheese. Microwave on high for 1 minute intervals, stirring each time, until cheese is melted.

Serve hot with tortilla or corn chips.

Game Day Cheese Dip

Makes 6 to 8 servings

1 8-ounce package cream cheese

2 cups grated Cheddar or Jalapeño Jack cheese

1 cup mayonnaise

1/4 cup finely chopped green onions

Preheat oven to 350 degrees. Coat a shallow microwave-safe baking dish with cooking spray.

Combine all ingredients in prepared dish. Microwave on high for about 2 minutes or until cheese is melted enough to blend smoothly. Stir until combined.

Place in oven and bake for 20 minutes or until lightly browned.

Serve with Fritos Scoops! or other corn chips.

Buffalo Chicken Dip

Makes 6 to 8 servings

2 8-ounce packages cream cheese, softened at room temperature

1 cup ranch dressing

3/4 cup pepper sauce such as Tabasco

2 cups shredded cooked white meat chicken

1 cup shredded Cheddar cheese

Preheat oven to 350 degrees. Coat a glass pie plate with cooking spray.

In a medium bowl, beat together cream cheese, ranch dressing, and pepper sauce. Fold in chicken.

Spread mixture into prepared pie plate. Bake for 15 minutes. Sprinkle cheese on top and bake 10 to 15 minutes longer.

Serve hot with corn chips.

CUCUMBER SALSA

Makes 2 cups

1 large cucumber, peeled, seeded, and finely chopped
1 large red bell pepper, seeded and finely chopped
1/2 cup finely chopped red onion
2 small jalapeños, seeded and finely chopped
2 tablespoons olive oil
1 tablespoon red wine vinegar
1/2 teaspoon salt
1/2 cup finely chopped cilantro

In a small bowl, combine the cucumber, bell pepper, onions, jalapeños, olive oil, vinegar, and salt. Cover and let stand at room temperature for 45 minutes, stirring a couple of times. Add the cilantro and adjust the seasonings just before serving.

Serve with corn or tortilla chips.

This "dip" is particularly delicious served with fresh grilled or roasted salmon.

Black Bean Salsa Dip

Makes 6 to 8 servings

1 15-ounce can black beans, drained and rinsed
2 15-ounce cans whole kernel corn, drained
Large tomato, peeled and chopped, to make 1 cup
2 tablespoons finely chopped red onion
1/4 cup finely chopped cilantro
1 jalapeño, seeded and finely chopped
1/2 cup balsamic vinegar
1/4 cup vegetable oil
1 1/2 tablespoons Dijon mustard
1/2 teaspoon salt
1/4 teaspoon fresh ground pepper

In a medium bowl, combine the beans, corn, tomato, onion, cilantro, and jalapeño; mix well.

In a jar with a lid, combine balsamic vinegar, oil, mustard, salt, and pepper. Close lid tightly and shake well.

Pour the vinegar mixture over the bean mixture and toss to coat. Marinate at room temperature for 2 hours or longer, stirring occasionally.

Serve with corn or tortilla chips.

Corn Chowder Dip

Makes 6 to 8 servings

1 11-ounce can white shoepeg corn, drained
2 tablespoons finely chopped green onions
16 ounces grated Cheddar cheese
4 jalapeños, seeded and finely chopped
1 cup mayonnaise
1/2 cup sour cream

In a small bowl, combine ingredients together, mixing well. Cover tightly with plastic wrap and chill several hours or overnight. Make 24 hours ahead for best flavor.

Serve with corn chips.

Texas Caviar

Makes 6 to 8 servings

1 16-ounce can black-eyed peas, drained
2 tomatoes, peeled and chopped
2 tablespoons finely chopped green onions
1 tablespoon chopped fresh cilantro
3 tablespoons fresh lime juice
1 tablespoon olive oil
2 cloves garlic, finely chopped
1/2 teaspoon ground cumin
1/4 teaspoon salt

Place peas in colander; rinse with cold water and drain.

In a medium bowl, combine drained peas with remaining ingredients, mixing well to coat. Cover tightly with plastic wrap and refrigerate several hours or overnight for best flavor.

Fruit Dip

Makes 6 to 8 servings

1 8-ounce package cream cheese, softened at room temperature
1 7-ounce jar marshmallow crème

Combine ingredients in small bowl. Using handheld electric mixer or spatula, blend ingredients until smooth.

Serve with berries or pieces of fresh fruit.

Appetizers/Snacks

TIP

To make radish flowers: Wash the radishes. Trim both ends. With a paring knife, cut four evenly spaced vertical slices halfway through the radish. Turn radish 90 degrees (one-quarter turn) and cut four more evenly spaced vertical slices crossways against the others. Place radishes in a sealed plastic bag with ice water for several minutes to several hours. This will "open" the radish and give it the appearance of a rose.

Jalapeño Poppers

Makes 24 poppers

12 fresh jalapeño peppers, cut in half and seeds removed
1 8-ounce package cream cheese, softened at room temperature
12 strips thin-sliced bacon, cut into two pieces of equal length
Picks as needed

Preheat oven to 425 degrees. Coat a baking sheet with cooking spray.

Spread a tablespoon of cream cheese in the middle of each jalapeño half. Wrap with 1/2 bacon strip and secure with a pick.

Place stuffed jalapeño halves on prepared baking sheet. Bake 40 to 45 minutes or until bacon is crisp.

Jalapeño Fudge

Makes 20 to 24 pieces

8 large eggs
4 cups grated sharp Cheddar cheese
6 fresh jalapeño peppers, stems and seeds removed, finely chopped

Preheat oven to 350 degrees. Grease bottom and sides of a 9" x 13" glass baking dish.

In a medium bowl, beat eggs until well-combined. Stir in cheese and jalapeños, mixing well. Pour into prepared baking dish.

Bake for 20 minutes or until edges start to brown and middle is firm. Cool for 10 to 15 minutes. Cut into 2" squares.

Easy and very tasty.

Holiday Meatballs

Makes 40 to 48 meatballs

2 eggs

1/2 cup milk

2 pounds ground beef

1 pound ground pork

1/2 cup finely chopped yellow onion

2 teaspoons garlic powder

2 cups oatmeal

1/2 cup ketchup

4 tablespoons Worcestershire sauce

2 teaspoons salt

2 teaspoons fresh ground pepper

4 tablespoons olive oil, divided use

4 tablespoons butter, divided use

2 12-ounce bottles chili sauce

1 14-ounce can whole berry cranberry sauce

1 14-ounce can jellied cranberry sauce

In a small bowl, whisk together the eggs and milk. In a large bowl, combine the beef, pork, onions, garlic powder, egg mixture, oatmeal, ketchup, Worcestershire sauce, salt, and pepper. With clean hands, knead mixture to combine. Shape into meatballs the size of a golf ball.

In a large skillet, heat 2 tablespoons each olive oil and butter over medium-high heat. Add the meatballs, browning on all sides. Do not crowd meatballs. If needed, brown meatballs in two batches. Remove drippings between batches, adding 2 tablespoons each oil and butter. Drain on paper towels.

Preheat oven to 300 degrees. In a medium bowl, combine chili and cranberry sauces. Pour over meatballs in heat-safe serving dish, tossing to coat thoroughly. Heat through, about 10 to 15 minutes, and serve.

These meatballs are delicious; make a big batch for a large party. Better yet, the meatballs may be made ahead of time and frozen. Heat meatballs in 300-degree oven to thaw. Combine with sauce just before serving.

Pepper Jack Cheese Wafers

Makes about 36 pieces

1 1/2 cups butter, softened at room temperature
16 ounces shredded jack cheese with peppers
4 cups flour
1 teaspoon salt

In a large bowl, beat together the butter and cheese with a hand mixer at medium speed until well-combined. In a medium bowl, combine flour and salt.

Using handheld mixer on low speed, gradually beat flour mixture into butter and cheese until well-combined. Shape dough into two 8″ logs. Wrap in waxed paper and refrigerator overnight.

Preheat oven to 350 degrees. Line flat or shallow baking sheets with parchment paper. Cut logs into 1/8″-thick slices. Place slices on parchment-lined baking sheets; sides should not touch.

Bake for 8 to 10 minutes or until edges of cheese wafers are lightly browned. Cool on pans or wire racks.

Store cheese wafers in airtight containers up to three days.

ASPARAGUS BEEF ROLL-UPS

Makes 36 pieces

Ice

2 cups water

36 fresh asparagus spears, tough ends trimmed

1 8-ounce carton spreadable chive and onion cream cheese

4 tablespoons prepared horseradish

2 5-ounce packages thinly sliced roast beef

Place a layer of ice in a 9″ x 13″ glass baking dish; set aside.

In a large skillet, bring the water to a boil over high heat. Add asparagus; cover and boil for 2 to 3 minutes or until crisp-tender. Drain and immediately place asparagus on ice, adding cold water to cover. Cool thoroughly, about 5 minutes.

Drain asparagus and pat dry. In a small bowl, combine the cream cheese and horseradish. Pat beef slices dry with paper towels. Spread each slice with a thin layer of cream cheese mixture; top with an asparagus spear. Roll up tightly. Refrigerate until serving.

Tortilla Roll-Ups

Makes about 60 pieces

2 8-ounce packages cream cheese, softened at room temperature

1 8-ounce carton sour cream

2 tablespoons picante sauce plus additional for serving

2 tablespoons finely chopped green onions

1 jalapeño pepper, stem and seeds removed, finely chopped

2 tablespoons lime juice

1 teaspoon Worcestershire sauce

1/2 teaspoon garlic salt

2 tablespoons bean dip (optional)

12 flour tortillas

In a medium bowl, using a handheld mixer on low speed, blend together all ingredients except the tortillas. Put 1 tablespoon of the mixture in center of each tortilla and spread evenly. Roll tightly and place seam side down with sides touching in a single layer in a shallow baking dish. Cover tightly with plastic wrap and refrigerate several hours or overnight.

When ready to serve, cut each tortilla roll into 1/2" pieces. Serve with additional picante sauce.

Deviled Eggs

Makes 12

6 hard-cooked eggs, peeled and sliced in half
1 teaspoon finely chopped sweet yellow onion
1 teaspoon sweet pickle relish
1/2 cup Miracle Whip salad dressing
1/2 teaspoon salt
1/2 teaspoon fresh ground pepper
1 tablespoon paprika

Separate yolks and place in a small bowl. Arrange egg whites on an egg tray.

Mash egg yolks with a fork or masher. Blend in remaining ingredients except paprika. Fill each egg white with about a teaspoon of yolk mixture. Dust with paprika.

Refrigerate several hours to chill thoroughly. Serve chilled.

This is an Easter favorite at our house.

Holiday Cheese Ball

Makes one large or two small balls

2 8-ounce packages cream cheese
1 8-ounce jar Cheez Whiz
1 5-ounce jar Kraft Roka blue cheese spread
4 ounces grated Cheddar cheese
3 tablespoons finely chopped green onions, tops only
2 tablespoons sour cream
2 tablespoons lemon juice
1 cup finely chopped pecans

Let all cheeses soften at room temperature. Blend together cheeses and remaining ingredients except pecans. Shape into one large or two smaller, equal-size balls and refrigerate until firm. Roll in nuts to coat.

Pigs in a Blanket

Makes 20 to 24 pieces

1 8-ounce package refrigerated crescent dinner rolls
1 12-ounce package little smokies sausages
1/3 cup whole-grain mustard

Preheat oven to 400 degrees. Line a baking sheet with parchment paper.

Separate pieces of crescent roll dough at perforations. Cut each piece into three triangles. Place a sausage at the wide edge of a triangle and roll to enclose sausage. Place sausage rolls on prepared baking sheet.

Bake for 15 to 20 minutes or until puffed and golden brown.

Serve with the mustard.

Pepperoni Pinwheels

Makes 20 pinwheels

1 8-ounce can refrigerated crescent dinner rolls
48 slices pepperoni
1/2 cup shredded mozzarella cheese
1 cup pizza or spaghetti sauce, heated through

Preheat oven to 350 degrees.

Separate dough into four rectangles. Sprinkle each rectangle with 2 tablespoons cheese and 12 slices of pepperoni. Starting at shortest side, tightly roll up each rectangle, pinching edges to seal. Slice each roll into five equal pinwheel slices.

Arrange pinwheels on ungreased cookie sheet. Bake for 18 to 20 minutes or until golden brown.

Serve pinwheels with warm pizza sauce.

Spinach Balls

Makes 24 to 30 pieces

1 10-ounce package frozen chopped spinach

1 1/2 cups herb-seasoned stuffing mix

3 tablespoons finely chopped onion

3 eggs, well-beaten

6 tablespoons butter, melted

1/4 cup grated Parmesan cheese

1 teaspoon fresh ground pepper

1 1/2 teaspoons garlic salt

Preheat oven to 325 degrees. Lightly grease a cookie sheet.

Cook spinach according to package directions; drain and squeeze in towels to remove excess moisture. In a medium bowl, combine spinach and the remaining ingredients, mixing well. Refrigerate 20 to 30 minutes.

Shape mixture into 3/4" balls and place on prepared cookie sheet. Bake for 15 to 20 minutes or until golden brown.

RATTLESNAKE BITES

Makes 24 pieces

1 tablespoon butter

1 pound lean ground beef

1 teaspoon garlic salt

2 tablespoons chopped green chilies

2 tablespoons finely chopped jalapeño peppers, stems and seeds removed

1 8-ounce package cream cheese, cubed

1/4 teaspoon ground cumin

1/4 teaspoon Gebhardt chili powder

3 8-ounce packages refrigerated crescent dinner rolls

Preheat oven to 375 degrees.

In a large skillet, melt the butter. Crumble beef and add to skillet along with garlic salt, green chilies, and jalapeños. Cook over medium heat until meat is no longer pink, stirring occasionally. Pour off excess grease. Stir in cream cheese, cumin, and chili powder, stirring to combine evenly. Cool slightly.

Meanwhile separate crescent dough into twenty-four triangles. Place 1 tablespoon of beef mixture along the short end of each triangle; carefully roll up. Place point side down 2 inches apart on ungreased baking sheets.

Bake for about 12 to 14 minutes or until golden brown. Serve warm.

Our family particularly enjoys these spicy nibbles while watching football games.

Praline Pecans

Makes 3 cups

1 cup sugar
1 cup packed brown sugar
1/2 cup water
2 tablespoons honey

1/2 teaspoon ground cinnamon
3 teaspoons vanilla
1/4 teaspoon rum extract
3 cups pecan halves

In a heavy saucepan, combine the sugars, water, honey, and cinnamon. Bring to a boil over medium heat; do not stir. Cook over medium heat until a candy thermometer reads 240 degrees. Remove from the heat; add extracts. Cool to lukewarm without stirring.

Beat with a handheld mixer for 2 to 3 minutes or until creamy. Stir in pecans, mixing until evenly coated. Quickly turn onto waxed paper in a single layer. Separate large clumps. Cool for several hours or until dry.

Popcorn Balls

Makes 15 to 18 popcorn balls

2 cups sugar
1/2 cup light corn syrup
1/2 cup water
1/2 teaspoon strawberry flavoring
Food coloring of choice
5 quarts popcorn, popped

In a medium saucepan, cook the sugar, corn syrup, and water over medium-high heat. Cook to hard boil or 245 degrees on a candy thermometer. Add strawberry flavoring and a couple of drops of desired food coloring. Spread popcorn on waxed paper on cookie sheets. Pour candy mixture over popcorn; stir with spoon. With butter on hands, form 3″ to 4″ balls. Cool on waxed paper.

Homemade Cheese Snack Crackers

Makes 60 crackers

8 ounces coarsely shredded extra-sharp Cheddar cheese

1/4 cup unsalted butter, softened at room temperature

1 teaspoon kosher salt

1 cup flour

2 tablespoons ice water

Preheat oven to 375 degrees. Line two baking sheets with parchment paper.

Using a stand mixer with paddle attachment, combine cheese, butter, and salt. Add flour and mix at low speed (dough will be pebbly). Slowly add the water and mix until dough is stiff and forms a ball.

Pat dough into a disk. Wrap in waxed paper; refrigerate for 1 hour. Divide dough into two portions; roll each portion to a very thin (1/8″) 10″ x 12″ rectangle. Using a fluted pastry cutter, cut dough into 1″ squares and transfer to parchment-lined baking sheets.

Bake for 15 to 17 minutes or until puffed and brown at the edges. Watch carefully to avoid burning, as all ovens cook differently. Immediately transfer crackers to wire racks to cool.

Patty's Party Mix

Makes 5 to 6 cups

1 12-ounce box Crispix cereal
2 cups pretzel sticks
10 tablespoons butter
10 tablespoons Worcestershire sauce

5 tablespoons lemon juice
3 tablespoons Lawry's seasoned salt
2 tablespoons garlic powder
2 tablespoons onion powder

Preheat oven to 250 degrees.

Mix cereal and pretzels in a 9″ x 13″ baking pan. Combine other ingredients in a small saucepan over medium heat and cook until butter is melted. Pour over cereal and pretzels, tossing to coat evenly.

Place in oven and bake for 1 hour, stirring every 15 minutes.

Puppy Chow

Makes 5 to 6 cups

3/4 cup peanut butter
1 cup semi-sweet chocolate chips
1/4 cup butter

1 12-ounce box Crispix cereal
2 cups powdered sugar

In a medium saucepan over medium heat, melt the peanut butter, chocolate chips, and butter together. Place cereal in a large kettle or bowl; add melted ingredients and stir well.

Pour the powdered sugar into a large brown paper bag or plastic food bag; add the chocolate and peanut butter-coated cereal. Fold the bag to seal and shake well to coat evenly.

You'll need a large paper or plastic food bag for easier preparation of this recipe.

Caramel Corn

Makes 12 servings

1 cup unpopped popcorn kernels to make about 8 quarts, popped

2 cups firmly packed dark brown sugar

1 cup butter

1/2 cup light corn syrup

2 teaspoons salt

1 teaspoon ground cinnamon

1 teaspoon baking soda

Preheat oven to 250 degrees.

Pop popcorn; remove and discard any unpopped kernels. Spread popcorn in a large roasting pan.

In a large saucepan, combine brown sugar, butter, corn syrup, salt, and cinnamon. Bring to a boil over medium-high heat, stirring constantly, and cook for 2 minutes. Remove from heat and stir in baking soda (mixture will foam).

Pour caramel mixture over popcorn, stirring gently to coat.

Bake for 1 hour, stirring every 10 minutes. Remove from oven and spread in a single layer on waxed paper. Cool completely and store in airtight container.

Soups

TIP

Use a food processor for any vegetables like onions, peppers, or celery. You will get more of a blended flavor, and if someone does not like something, they will not know it is in the recipe.

Taco Soup

Makes 10 to 12 servings

1 pound lean ground beef
2 tablespoons vegetable oil
1/2 onion, finely chopped
3 cloves garlic, finely chopped
1 teaspoon salt
3 tablespoons Gebhardt chili powder
1 teaspoon chipotle chili powder
1 teaspoon ground cumin
2 15-ounce cans whole peeled tomatoes, crushed
1 10-ounce can Rotel diced tomatoes and green chilies
2 6-ounce cans tomato paste
1 16-ounce can chili beans, drained
1 15-ounce can whole kernel corn, drained
1 1-ounce package Hidden Valley Ranch Salad Dressing and Seasoning Mix
1 12-ounce package white or yellow corn tortillas, halved and sliced into thin strips (may substitute crumbled tortilla chips)
6 tablespoons vegetable oil, divided use

Brown meat in a large stockpot with the oil over medium-high heat. Add onion, garlic, and salt. When meat is browned, add chili powders and cumin, stirring to coat the meat. Add remaining ingredients; bring to a boil. Lower heat and simmer for 1 hour or until flavors blend, stirring often.

If using tortillas, heat 3 tablespoons of the oil in a medium skillet over medium-high heat. Add half the tortilla strips and fry until crisp, 2 to 3 minutes. If needed, add additional oil and cook second batch of tortilla strips until crisp. Omit this step if using crumbled tortilla chips.

Our family enjoys this delicious soup every Halloween.

Chicken Tortilla Soup

Makes 10 to 12 servings

4 chicken breasts, skinless and boneless
Water, as needed
1 tablespoon olive oil
3 tablespoons finely chopped red onion
3 cloves garlic, finely chopped
1 jalapeño pepper, seeded and finely chopped
1 teaspoon salt
2 teaspoons Gebhardt chili powder
1/2 teaspoon ground cumin
1 teaspoon ground oregano
2 15-ounce cans chicken broth
1 15-ounce can diced tomatoes, undrained
1 10-ounce can Rotel diced tomatoes and green chilies, undrained
1 15-ounce can whole kernel corn, drained
1/4 cup chopped fresh cilantro
12 corn tortillas, halved and sliced into thin strips
3 tablespoons vegetable oil
1 avocado, peeled, seeded, and sliced
1 cup shredded Monterey Jack cheese
1 cup sour cream

Place chicken breasts in a medium saucepan with just enough water to cover. Bring water to a boil, lower heat, cover, and simmer until tender, about 30 minutes. Remove chicken from stock and let cool enough to handle. Reserve 1 cup cooking liquid. Cut chicken into bite-size pieces.

In a large stockpot, heat olive oil over medium-high heat. Cook onion and garlic for 2 to 3 minutes; stir in the salt, chili powder, cumin, oregano, jalapeño pepper, tomatoes, tomatoes with chilies, broth, corn, cilantro, and reserved cooking liquid. Reduce heat and simmer for 30 to 45 minutes to blend flavors.

Separate tortilla pieces. In a medium skillet, heat vegetable oil over medium-high heat. Fry tortillas strips, stirring to coat and cook until crisp and browned.

Serve with garnishes: tortilla strips, avocado slices, cheese, and sour cream.

Texas Chili

Makes 8 to 10 servings

1 pound lean ground beef

2 tablespoons vegetable oil

1/2 onion, finely chopped

3 cloves garlic, finely chopped

1 teaspoon salt

3 tablespoons Gebhardt chili powder

1 teaspoon chipotle chili powder

1 teaspoon ground cumin

2 15-ounce cans diced tomatoes, undrained

1 10-ounce can Rotel diced tomatoes and green chilies, undrained

2 6-ounce cans tomato paste

1 16-ounce can pinto beans, rinsed and drained (optional)

In a large stockpot over medium high heat, add oil and cook meat until brown. Add onion, garlic, and salt; cook until onion is soft. Stir in chili powders and cumin to evenly coat the meat.

Add tomatoes with chilies, tomatoes, and tomato paste; bring to a boil. Reduce heat, cover, and simmer for 1 hour or until flavors blend, stirring often. If desired, stir in beans.

Baked Potato Soup

Makes 6 to 8 servings

1/2 cup butter

1 1/2 quarts (6 cups) milk

3/4 cup flour

1 teaspoon salt

1 teaspoon fresh ground pepper

4 large Yukon Gold potatoes, peeled and cut into bite-size cubes

4 green onions, sliced and finely chopped, divided use

3/4 pound bacon, cooked crisp, drained and crumbled, divided use

1 cup sour cream

1 cup shredded Cheddar cheese

In a large saucepan or Dutch oven, melt butter over medium heat. Stir in milk. Slowly add flour, whisking constantly. Stir in the salt and pepper.

When milk mixture is hot, add potatoes, onions, and 1/2 cup bacon. Simmer over low heat for 45 to 60 minutes or until potatoes are fork tender. Garnish with the reserved bacon, sour cream, and cheese.

Bourbon Street Corn and Crab Bisque

Makes 8 to 10 servings

1/3 cup flour

1/3 cup butter

2 tablespoons finely chopped garlic

1/3 cup sliced, finely chopped green onions

1/3 cup finely chopped parsley

2 tablespoons Cajun seasoning blend

3 cups chicken stock, heated to boiling

1 teaspoon liquid shrimp and crab boil seasoning or to taste

6 ears fresh corn, cut off the cob

1 quart heavy cream

1 pound fresh crabmeat

1/2 teaspoon salt

1/2 teaspoon fresh ground pepper

Put corn in a large stockpot and cover with the broth. Bring to a boil and add the garlic. Add the seasonings, shrimp and crab boil, and the green onions. Reduce to simmer for about 30 minutes.

In another medium saucepan, make a roux with equal parts of butter and flour to desired color; add to your simmering pot. Adjust thickness with stock. Add cream and heat to almost a boil. Add crab and cook about 5 minutes.

Serve with sliced baguettes.

This is a real crowd pleaser, especially served with sliced baguettes.

Spicy Chicken Chili

Makes 6 to 8 servings

2 tablespoons butter

1 1/2 cups finely chopped sweet yellow onion

1 cup finely chopped green bell pepper

3 jalapeño peppers, stems removed, seeded, and finely chopped

3 cloves garlic, finely chopped

2 tablespoons Gebhardt chili powder

2 teaspoons ground cumin

1/2 teaspoon ground oregano

4 cups cooked chicken breast, cut into bite-size pieces

1 cup water

1/2 teaspoon ground red (cayenne) pepper

1/3 teaspoon fresh ground pepper

1 tablespoon Worcestershire sauce

1 tablespoon Dijon mustard

1 15-ounce can stewed tomatoes, undrained

1 15-ounce can chicken broth

1 12-ounce bottle chili sauce

1 16-ounce can great northern beans, drained

1 16-ounce can whole kernel corn, drained

Optional garnishes: sour cream, sliced avocadoes, and shredded cheese

In large stockpot, melt butter over medium heat until hot. Add onion, peppers, and garlic; cook for 5 minutes or until onion is soft. Add chili powder, cumin, and oregano; cook 2 minutes longer. Add chicken, stirring to coat well. Stir in water and remaining ingredients except beans and corn; bring to a boil. Cover, reduce heat, and simmer for an hour to blend flavors. Add beans and corn; simmer an additional 10 minutes.

Serve with desired garnishes.

Corn Chowder

Makes 10 to 12 servings

8 slices bacon

1/2 cup finely chopped onion

2 cloves garlic, finely chopped

2 teaspoons salt

1/2 teaspoon paprika

1/4 teaspoon crushed red pepper

1/4 teaspoon fresh ground pepper

2 10-ounce packages frozen whole kernel corn

3 cups chicken broth

1 10.5-ounce can condensed cream of chicken soup

1 cup half-and-half

In large saucepan, cook bacon until crisp; drain on paper towels. With a slotted spoon, remove to a paper towel lined plate. Reserve drippings in saucepan. Over medium heat, add the onions and garlic to bacon drippings. Cook for 5 to 7 minutes until onion begins to brown. Add the paprika, salt, pepper, and red pepper, stirring for 2 minutes. Stir in the corn, broth, cream of chicken soup, and half-and-half; bring to a boil. Reduce heat and cover and simmer for 15 to 20 minutes. Adjust seasoning with salt and pepper if desired.

Garnish each serving with crumbled bacon.

New Mexico Cheese and Potato Soup

Makes 10 to 12 servings

1 pound bacon, cut into bite-size pieces
1/2 cup finely chopped white onion
1/2 cup finely chopped celery
2 cloves garlic, finely chopped
2 tablespoons flour
4 cups russet potatoes, peeled and cut into bite-size cubes
1/3 cup chopped green chilies
1 tablespoon dry mustard
2 teaspoons paprika
3 cups chicken broth
1 tablespoon Worcestershire sauce
1/2 teaspoon Tabasco sauce
2 cups cooked chicken breast, shredded
1 cup shredded longhorn Cheddar cheese
2 cups shredded jalapeño jack cheese
2 cups half-and-half
1 teaspoon salt
1 teaspoon fresh ground pepper
1/8 teaspoon ground red (cayenne) pepper
3 tablespoons vegetable oil or as needed
1 12-ounce package white or yellow corn tortillas, halved and cut into thin strips
2 green onions, sliced and finely chopped

Cook bacon in a large saucepan over medium-high heat until crisp. With a slotted spoon, remove to a paper towel lined plate. Reserve drippings in saucepan. Add white onion, celery, and garlic to drippings and cook until onion is softened, about 5 minutes.

Stir in flour and cook 1 to 2 minutes. Add potatoes, green chilies, dry mustard, and paprika; cook, stirring to coat potatoes, about 1 minute. Stir in broth, Worcestershire sauce, and Tabasco. Bring to a boil, reduce heat to medium-low, and cook until potatoes are soft, about 10 to 15 minutes.

Using the back of a spoon or potato masher, coarsely mash potatoes; then stir in cheese and half-and-half until the cheese is melted, about 2 minutes. Remove soup from heat; add salt, cayenne, and pepper to taste.

In medium skillet, heat oil over medium-high heat. Add half the tortilla strips and fry until crisp, 2 to 3 minutes. If needed, add additional oil and cook second batch of tortilla strips until crisp.

Garnish with bacon, tortilla strips, and green onions.

Grandma Lane's Chicken and Dumplings

Makes 6 to 8 servings

6 chicken breasts, boneless and skinless
4 cups water
4 tablespoons butter
2 cups chicken broth
1 teaspoon salt
1/2 teaspoon fresh ground pepper
Flour as needed
2 7.5-ounce cans buttermilk homestyle biscuits (not flaky)
4 cups milk

In large saucepan, combine chicken breasts, water, butter, broth, salt, and pepper. Bring to a boil, reduce heat, and simmer until chicken is tender, about 25 to 30 minutes. Remove chicken and cool enough to handle. Pour broth through fine strainer to remove solids.

Dust a pastry sheet or large cutting board and rolling pin with a light coating of flour. Place biscuits on floured surface. Using floured rolling pin, roll out each biscuit until very thin. Use additional flour as needed to prevent biscuits from sticking. Slice each rolled biscuit into strips and then into smaller squares.

Return strained broth and chicken to clean saucepan over high heat and bring to a boil. Reduce heat to low and add milk slowly, stirring often. Slide pieces of dough into hot liquid, a few at a time, stirring constantly. Cook for 15 to 20 minutes until mixture thickens and dumplings are not mushy, no longer doughy. Adjust consistency as needed with additional broth or milk.

This rich dish is a particular favorite with our family.

Mom's Chicken Soup

Makes 10 to 12 servings

4 chicken breasts, boneless and skinless

1 quart water

2 15-ounce cans chicken broth

1 teaspoon salt

1 teaspoon fresh ground pepper

3 whole black peppercorns

1/3 cup finely chopped onion

6 celery stalks, finely chopped

6 carrots, peeled and sliced thin

1 cup fine egg noodles, cooked, to make about 2 cups

1/4 cup finely chopped fresh parsley

In a large Dutch oven or stockpot, combine chicken, water, broth, salt, pepper, and peppercorns. Bring to a boil over medium-high heat, lower heat, and simmer until chicken is tender, about 25 to 30 minutes. Remove chicken, let cool enough to handle, and cut into bite-size pieces.

Pour cooking liquid juices through a fine strainer to remove solids. Return to clean pot and add onion, celery, and carrots. Cover and bring to a boil. Reduce heat to simmer and cook until vegetables are tender, about 10 minutes. Add cooked noodles and parsley; heat through.

We also call this "get well soup."

Pasta e Fagioli Soup (Italian Pasta and Bean Soup)

Makes 6 to 8 servings

1 tablespoon olive oil

1/2 cup finely chopped onion

3 ounces pancetta or bacon, finely chopped

3 cloves garlic, finely chopped

3/4 cup dry red wine

2 15-ounce cans white kidney beans, rinsed and drained

2 15-ounce cans chicken broth

1 14.5-ounce can chopped tomatoes

1 teaspoon salt

1/2 teaspoon crushed red pepper

1 1-pound package ditalini pasta or elbow macaroni

1/4 cup chopped fresh basil

2 tablespoons dried oregano

1 tablespoon grated Parmesan cheese (optional)

In a Dutch oven or large saucepan, heat the oil over medium heat. Add the onion, pancetta or bacon, and garlic. Cook for about 5 minutes or until onion is tender and pancetta or bacon is brown and crisp, stirring occasionally.

Add wine, stirring to scrape up any crusty brown bits on bottom of pan. Stir in beans, broth, tomatoes, salt, and crushed red pepper. Bring to a boil and reduce heat. Simmer, covered, for 20 minutes.

Meanwhile cook pasta according to package directions; drain. Stir cooked pasta, basil, and oregano into soup mixture and cook for about 5 more minutes or until heated through.

Garnish with cheese, if desired.

New Orleans Gumbo

Makes 6 to 8 servings

2 tablespoons vegetable oil

2 tablespoons butter

4 tablespoons flour

1/2 cup finely chopped sweet yellow onion

1 cup finely chopped celery

3 cloves garlic, finely chopped

1 6-ounce can tomato paste

1 14.5-ounce can chopped tomatoes, undrained

1 quart water

2 bay leaves

1/2 teaspoon dried thyme

1/8 teaspoon Accent (monosodium glutamate)

2 tablespoons dried parsley

1 teaspoon salt

1/2 teaspoon fresh ground pepper

1 pound fresh small shrimp, shelled and deveined

1 cup fresh crabmeat

1 tablespoon gumbo filé powder

1 cup rice, cooked to make about 2 cups

In a Dutch oven or large stockpot, combine the butter and the oil over medium heat and melt butter. Add the flour and cook until brown, stirring constantly. Add onion, celery, and garlic; stir and cook 2 to 3 minutes until onion begins to soften.

Stir in tomato paste and tomatoes. Add water, bay leaves, thyme, Accent, parsley, salt, and pepper. Bring to a boil, lower heat, and simmer for 30 minutes. Add shrimp and cook 10 minutes; stir in crabmeat and gumbo filé powder. Heat through.

Serve over cooked rice.

Salads

TIP

A hard-boiled egg takes about 20 minutes to cook. Boiled potatoes take about 25 to 30 minutes or until soft when pierced with a fork. Cover both with water in the appropriate size saucepan and cook over medium-high heat.

Caesar Salad

Makes 4 to 6 servings

1 clove garlic, peeled and crushed

1 2-ounce can flat fillets of anchovies, drained (optional)

1/4 teaspoon prepared mustard

1/2 teaspoon Worcestershire sauce

1 raw egg

1/2 cup olive oil

1/4 cup white wine vinegar

1/2 teaspoon fresh ground pepper

1 head romaine lettuce, rinsed, dried, and torn into bite-size pieces

2 tablespoons grated Parmesan cheese

In large wooden salad bowl, mash garlic clove with back of a fork. If using anchovies, finely chop and crush. Combine anchovies with garlic and mash together. Mix the mustard and Worcestershire sauce into garlic mixture. Whisk in raw egg, beating well until mixture is thoroughly combined and thickened. Gradually whisk in oil and vinegar; season with pepper. Mix well. Add lettuce, tossing well to coat evenly with dressing. Sprinkle with cheese before serving.

Garden Salad with Ranchy Vinaigrette

Makes 8 to 10 servings

1 1-ounce package Hidden Valley Ranch Salad Dressing and Seasoning Mix

1/4 cup extra-virgin olive oil

3 tablespoons white wine vinegar

2 heads iceberg lettuce, rinsed, dried, and torn into bite-size pieces

1 cup shredded carrots

1/2 cup grape tomato halves

1/2 cup cucumber slices (cut into half-moons)

In salad bowl, whisk together ranch salad dressing mix, oil, and vinegar until smooth; set aside.

Just before serving, add lettuce, carrots, tomatoes, and cucumber, tossing to combine evenly and coat with vinaigrette.

This is very easy but looks homemade.

Strawberry Romaine Salad

Makes 6 to 8 servings

1 cup salad oil

3/4 cup sugar

1/2 cup red wine vinegar

2 cloves garlic, finely chopped

1/2 teaspoon salt

1/2 teaspoon paprika

1/4 teaspoon ground white pepper

1 large head romaine lettuce, rinsed and torn into bite-size pieces

1 head Boston lettuce, rinsed and torn into bite-size pieces

1 cup shredded Monterey Jack cheese, optional

1 cup pecans, roasted

1 pint strawberries

1 medium red onion, sliced thin

In a jar with a lid, mix together the oil, sugar, vinegar, garlic, salt, paprika, and pepper. Shake well and refrigerate.

When ready to serve, combine lettuces, cheese, nuts, strawberries, and onion in large salad bowl. Add enough dressing to coat ingredients and toss to combine.

TACO SALAD

Makes 6 to 8 servings

1 tablespoon vegetable oil
2 tablespoons finely chopped red onion
1/2 teaspoon garlic salt
1/2 pound lean ground beef
1 tablespoon chili powder
1 15-ounce can ranch-style beans, drained and rinsed
1 head iceberg lettuce, rinsed, dried, and torn into bite-size pieces
1 medium red onion, sliced
1 cup grated Cheddar cheese
2 tomatoes, chopped
1/2 cup (or to taste) bottled Catalina or chipotle ranch salad dressing
1 cup tortilla chips, crumbled
1 avocado, peeled, seeded, and chopped (optional)

In a medium skillet, heat oil over medium-high heat. Add onion and garlic salt; cook for about a minute. Add meat, stirring to break into pieces; cook until browned. Add chili powder and stir to coat the meat. Remove from heat and cool slightly.

In large salad bowl, toss together beans, lettuce, onion, Cheddar cheese, and tomatoes. Stir in beef. Pour salad dressing over ingredients, tossing well to combine. Garnish with avocado and tortilla chips.

CLASSIC CHICKEN SALAD

Makes 4 to 6 servings

2 cups shredded cooked chicken breast
2 tablespoons finely chopped green onions
2 tablespoons finely chopped celery
1 cup mayonnaise
1 teaspoon salt
1/2 teaspoon fresh ground pepper
4 to 6 croissants, split
Lettuce leaves
Sliced tomatoes

In a medium bowl, combine all ingredients, mixing well. Adjust seasonings and mayonnaise to taste. Cover tightly and refrigerate several hours to chill and blend flavors.

For chicken salad sandwiches, serve on croissants with lettuce leaves and tomatoes.

Warm Honey Dijon Chicken Salad

Makes 4 to 6 servings

3/4 cup mayonnaise

1/4 cup honey

1/4 cup Dijon mustard

1/2 teaspoon dried tarragon leaves

4 chicken breasts, boneless and skinless

6 cups bite-size pieces of assorted salad greens

1/2 cup thinly sliced red onion

6 radishes, ends trimmed, sliced thin

In a jar with a lid, combine mayonnaise, honey, mustard, and tarragon. Shake well to blend; reserve 1/2 cup and refrigerate.

Place chicken in a shallow baking dish. Pour remaining mayonnaise mixture over chicken and cover tightly with plastic wrap. Refrigerate at least 20 minutes up to several hours or overnight to marinate. Drain; discard marinade.

Light charcoal or heat a gas grill to medium. Grill chicken, turning once, until chicken is cooked through, about 8 to 10 minutes. Juices should run clear when breast meat is pierced with a fork. Remove from grill.

In large salad bowl, combine salad greens with onion and radishes. Toss with reserved mayonnaise mixture, coating pieces evenly. Slice chicken into strips; arrange over greens. Serve immediately.

Thai Chicken Salad with Peanut Dressing

Makes 4 servings

2 cups shredded rotisserie chicken breast, skin and bones discarded

6 cups bite-size pieces romaine lettuce

1 cup shredded carrots

1/2 cup thinly sliced celery

2/3 cup light coconut milk

1 tablespoon brown sugar

2 tablespoons creamy peanut butter

1 tablespoon fresh lime juice

2 tablespoons soy sauce

1/8 teaspoon ground red (cayenne) pepper

In a large bowl, combine chicken, lettuce, carrots, and celery.

Combine remaining ingredients in a small saucepan over medium to high heat, stirring frequently. When mixture bubbles, reduce heat and simmer 5 minutes or until the mixture thickens slightly, stirring occasionally. Remove pan from heat and let cool 2 minutes. Pour warm dressing over the lettuce mixture; toss and serve.

Tuna Salad

Makes 4 to 6 servings

2 5-ounce cans solid white albacore tuna

1 tablespoon finely chopped red onion

2 tablespoons sweet pickle relish

1 teaspoon relish juice

1 hard-cooked egg, peeled and crushed with fork

1/2 teaspoon salt

1/4 teaspoon fresh ground pepper

1 cup Miracle Whip salad dressing

1/2 apple, peeled and chopped, optional

Drain tuna. Place in a medium bowl, breaking apart with a fork. Blend in remaining ingredients. Cover tightly and refrigerate several hours until chilled and flavors are well-blended.

Patty's Potato Salad

Makes 8 to 10 servings

8 large Yukon Gold or red potatoes

3 hard-cooked eggs, peeled and crushed with fork

1/4 cup finely chopped red onion

1/4 cup finely chopped sweet relish

1 teaspoon relish juice

2 cups Miracle Whip salad dressing

1 teaspoon salt

1 teaspoon fresh ground pepper

1/2 teaspoon paprika

In a large stockpot over medium-high heat, add enough cold water to cover potatoes. Bring to a boil over high heat; lower heat and simmer until fork tender, about 30 minutes. Drain and cool enough to handle.

Peel potatoes and cut into bite-size pieces; place in large salad bowl. If some pieces crumble, this is okay. Add eggs to potatoes. Blend in onion, relish, relish juice, Miracle Whip, salt, and pepper. Stir slowly but mix well. Add more salt or pepper or Miracle Whip to taste. Sprinkle with paprika.

Another Hensel family favorite.

Old-Fashioned German Potato Salad

Makes 6 to 8 servings

12 to 14 large new potatoes, unpeeled

1/2 cup sugar

1 teaspoon salt

1/2 teaspoon fresh ground pepper

1 teaspoon dry mustard

1/2 cup vegetable oil

1 cup white wine vinegar

1 cup chicken broth

3 tablespoons finely chopped green onions

2 tablespoons finely chopped fresh parsley

In large saucepan, add potatoes and enough water to cover. Over high heat, bring water to a boil. Reduce heat and simmer until potatoes are easily pierced with a fork, about 20 to 25 minutes. Cool enough to handle and peel while warm. Set aside.

In small saucepan, combine sugar, salt, pepper, dry mustard, oil, vinegar, and broth, stirring well. Place over medium heat and bring just to a boil, stirring until sugar is well-dissolved. Remove from heat.

Slice potatoes thin and place in a large bowl. Add just enough warm dressing to moisten potatoes. Gently blend in onions and parsley.

May be served warm or chilled.

Primavera Salad

Makes 6 to 8 servings

1 16-ounce package bow tie pasta, cooked according to package directions

2 beefsteak tomatoes, peeled, seeded, and chopped into small cubes

1 pound smoked turkey breast, sliced and chopped into bite-size pieces

2 tablespoons finely chopped green onions

2 tablespoons chopped fresh basil

2 tablespoons chopped fresh parsley

2/3 cup vegetable oil

1/4 cup water

1/4 cup white wine vinegar

1 tablespoon salt

1 tablespoon fresh ground pepper

1 finely chopped clove garlic

In large bowl, combine cooked pasta with tomatoes and turkey.

Using a large jar with lid or medium bowl and whisk, mix remaining ingredients. With lid on tightly, shake ingredients in jar or whisk together until well-combined.

Pour over pasta and tomatoes. Cover tightly and refrigerate overnight to blend flavors.

This is a delicious summertime salad.

Macaroni Salad

Make 6 to 8 servings

1 16-ounce package elbow macaroni
3 tablespoons sweet pickle relish
1 teaspoon relish juice
3 tablespoons finely chopped red onion
3 hard-cooked eggs, shelled and finely chopped
1 teaspoon celery seed
1 cup Miracle Whip salad dressing
1/2 teaspoon salt
1/2 teaspoon freshly ground pepper

Cook macaroni according to package directions; drain.

In large bowl, combine pasta with remaining ingredients; mix well. Adjust seasoning with salt and pepper to taste. Cover tightly and refrigerate several hours before serving.

Grandma's Old-Fashioned Cole Slaw

Makes 8 to 10 servings

1 medium head cabbage, shredded
1/2 cup finely chopped carrot
1/2 cup finely chopped green pepper
1/4 cup finely chopped red onion
1 cup plus 2 tablespoons sugar, divided use
1 cup vinegar
3/4 cup vegetable oil
1 tablespoon salt
1 tablespoon dry mustard
1 tablespoon celery seed

In a large bowl, combine cabbage, carrot, green pepper, and onion. Pour 1 cup sugar over all, but do not stir.

In a medium saucepan, combine remaining 2 tablespoons sugar and remaining ingredients. Bring to a rolling boil over high heat, stirring to dissolve sugar.

Pour over cabbage and mix well to blend. Cover tightly and refrigerate several hours or overnight to chill thoroughly and blend flavors. Stir well before serving.

Momo's Cabbage Slaw

Makes 6 to 8 servings

1/2 cup sugar
1/2 cup vegetable oil
1/2 cup white vinegar
1 teaspoon yellow mustard
1 teaspoon celery seed
1 teaspoon salt
1 teaspoon fresh ground pepper
1 medium head cabbage, shredded
1 medium green bell pepper, stem and seeds removed, finely chopped
1/2 cup finely chopped sweet yellow onion

In a medium size saucepan, combine sugar, oil, vinegar, mustard, celery seed, salt, and pepper. Bring to a boil over high heat, lower heat slightly, and cook for 3 to 4 minutes. Remove from heat.

In a large bowl, toss together cabbage, peppers, and onion.

Pour boiled dressing over cabbage mixture, mixing to coat evenly. May be served warm or chilled.

Momo's Cucumber Salad

Makes 4 to 6 servings

3 cucumbers, peeled and sliced thin
1 red onion, sliced thin
2 large beefsteak or East Texas tomatoes, peeled, seeded, and coarsely chopped
1/2 cup sugar
1 cup water
1 cup red wine vinegar
1 cup vegetable oil
1 tablespoons salt
1 tablespoon fresh ground pepper

In large bowl, toss together cucumbers, onion, and tomatoes.

In a jar with tight-fitting lid, combine sugar, water, vinegar, oil, salt, and pepper. Secure lid and shake well to blend.

Pour dressing over cucumbers. Cover tightly and marinate several hours or overnight to blend flavors.

Aunt Meta's Heavenly Holiday Salad

Makes 6 to 8 servings

1 1/2 cups pineapple juice
1 3-ounce package lime-flavored gelatin
1 3-ounce package cream cheese, softened
1 8-ounce can crushed pineapple, drained
1/2 cup chopped pecans
1 cup heavy whipping cream
Additional whipped cream for garnish

In a medium saucepan, bring the juice to a boil. Dissolve the gelatin in the juice and let cool.

In a medium bowl, cream the cream cheese with a handheld mixer until it is fluffy. Add the heavy whipping cream and cream together. Pour the juice and gelatin into the cheese mixture and mix well. Pour into a glass bowl or gelatin mold and chill for 5 to 6 hours. Garnish with whip cream.

7 Up Salad

Makes about 6 to 8 servings

1 8-ounce can crushed pineapple
1 cup hot water
1 3-ounce package lime-flavored gelatin
1 8-ounce package cream cheese,
  softened at room temperature
1 tablespoon sugar
1 teaspoon vanilla
1 12-ounce can 7 Up

Drain pineapple, reserving the juice in a 1-cup measure. Add enough water to make 1 cup. Pour liquid into a medium saucepan. Bring to a boil over medium-high heat. When liquid boils, pour into medium bowl, stirring in gelatin and cream cheese.

Using handheld mixer, beat mixture together at medium speed about 2 minutes until smooth. Add sugar, vanilla, and 7 Up. Blend on high speed for 1 minute. Add pineapple and mix 1 minute on low speed.

Pour into a glass dish or mold. Chill in refrigerator for 5 to 6 hours or overnight.

"Pink Stuff" Salad

Makes 8 to 10 servings

1 10-ounce jar maraschino cherries

1 8-ounce package cream cheese, softened at room temperature

1 20-ounce can crushed pineapple, drained

3 bananas, peeled and sliced

1 10.5-ounce bag miniature marshmallows

1 8-ounce tub Cool Whip whipped topping, thawed

Drain cherry juice into a medium bowl. Cut cherries in half.

Using handheld mixer, blend together cream cheese and cherry juice. Fold in cherries, pineapple, bananas, and marshmallows, evenly distributing ingredients. Fold in whipped topping. Cover tightly and refrigerate overnight.

This is a "must" on the Hensel holiday table.

Cranberry Orange Relish

Makes 4 cups

1 16-ounce bag fresh cranberries

2 cups sugar

1 teaspoon grated orange peel

1 1/2 cups orange juice

In a medium saucepan, combine ingredients and bring to a boil over medium-high heat. Lower heat and simmer for 10 minutes, stirring occasionally. Remove from heat and let cool.

Cover tightly and store in refrigerator.

Fruit Salad

Makes 6 to 8 servings

2 cups cantaloupe, cut into chunks
2 cups seedless red or green grapes, cut in half
2 cups seedless watermelon, cut into chunks
1 teaspoon finely chopped shredded lime peel
1/3 cup fresh lime juice
1 tablespoon chopped fresh mint
2 tablespoons honey
2 bananas, peeled and sliced
Fresh mint sprigs for garnish

Combine cantaloupe, grapes, and watermelon in a large glass bowl.

In a small bowl, whisk together zest, lime juice, chopped mint, and honey. Pour over fruit mixture. Stir in bananas just before serving. Garnish with mint sprigs.

Rum-Spiked Grilled Pineapple

Makes 6 servings

1 whole pineapple, peeled, cored, and cut in half lengthwise
2 tablespoons butter, melted
1/4 cup packed light brown sugar
1/4 cup dark rum
1/4 teaspoon ground cinnamon

Slice each pineapple half into six half-moons. Brush pineapple on both sides with melted butter.

Combine brown sugar, rum, and cinnamon in a microwave-safe bowl. Microwave on high 90 seconds or until sugar dissolves, stirring once during cooking.

Brush hot rum mixture evenly over pineapple wedges. Place pineapple on grill rack coated with cooking spray over medium hot coals. Grill 3 minutes on each side or until grill marks form and pineapple is glazed.

Red Hot Peaches

Makes 4 servings

1 15-ounce can peach halves
4 tablespoons Red Hots (cinnamon candy) or as needed
4 teaspoons lemon juice

Drain peaches; then place cut-side up in shallow dish. Fill empty pit of each peach half with a tablespoon of cinnamon candies. Add 1 teaspoon lemon juice per peach on top of candies.

Cover tightly and refrigerate 6 to 8 hours or overnight.

This pretty peach dish makes a great garnish for any meat or poultry entrée, such as Teriyaki chicken or steak. Delicious and easy to prepare, it should be made a day in advance of serving, as the lemon juice dissolves the candy.

Dressings, Marinades, and Sauces

TIP

The Opal apple, a yellow apple that resists browning when sliced, is the result of a cross between Golden Delicious and Topaz varieties. That makes it a great choice for salads or packing in lunches.

Balsamic Vinaigrette

Makes 2 1/4 cups

1/2 cup balsamic vinegar, preferably from Modena, Italy

1/4 cup pure maple syrup

1/4 cup finely chopped shallot

1 cup vegetable oil

1/2 cup olive oil

1/2 teaspoon salt

1/2 teaspoon fresh ground pepper

Place all ingredients in a large jar with a tight-fitting lid. Shake to mix and refrigerate. Shake before serving.

Vinaigrette

Makes about 1 cup

1 tablespoon Dijon mustard

4 tablespoons red wine vinegar

1 teaspoon sugar

1/2 teaspoon salt

1/2 teaspoon fresh ground pepper

2 cloves garlic, finely chopped

1 tablespoon finely chopped fresh parsley

1/2 cup olive oil

In a small bowl, stir together all ingredients except oil. Whisking constantly, add oil until all ingredients are well-combined.

Honey Mustard Dressing

Makes 2 quarts

2/3 cup honey

1 quart mayonnaise

1/8 teaspoon ground red (cayenne) pepper

1/2 teaspoon onion salt

2/3 cup mustard

2/3 cup vegetable oil

1/4 cup apple cider vinegar

Place honey in microwave-safe container and warm to a thinner, mixable consistency. In large bowl, combine warm honey with remaining ingredients, whisking to mix well. Cover tightly and store in refrigerator.

Russian Dressing

Makes about 2 cups

1 tablespoon finely chopped red bell pepper

1 tablespoon finely chopped green bell pepper

1 tablespoon finely chopped yellow onion

1/2 cup mayonnaise

1/4 cup ketchup

1 tablespoon Worcestershire sauce

2 tablespoons red wine vinegar

1 tablespoon champagne vinegar

Salt and pepper to taste

In a small bowl, whisk together all ingredients. Cover tightly and store in refrigerator.

Compared to some dressings, this one is a little more involved, but it is amazing.

Hot Bacon Dressing

Makes about 2 1/2 cups

- 1 16-ounce package thinly sliced bacon
- 1/4 cup chopped green onions
- 1/2 cup cider vinegar
- 1 cup water
- 3/4 cup sugar
- 1 tablespoon Dijon mustard
- 1/2 teaspoon salt
- 1/4 teaspoon fresh ground pepper
- 1 1/2 tablespoons cornstarch
- 1 tablespoon cold water

In a large skillet, cook bacon until crisp over medium heat. Drain on paper towels. When bacon is cool enough to handle, crumble into bite-size pieces. Set aside.

Reserve 2 tablespoons of drippings in the skillet. Add onion and sauté until tender, 3 to 5 minutes; remove from heat. Add vinegar, water, sugar, mustard, salt, pepper, and bacon; mix well.

In small bowl, stir together cornstarch and cold water until smooth. Stir cornstarch mixture into skillet. Return to heat, stirring until mixture comes to a boil. Cook for 2 minutes longer or until thickened, stirring constantly.

Serve warm over fresh spinach or mixed greens.

This is a great flavor combination for spinach salad.

Poppy Seed Dressing

Makes 2 cups

2/3 cup sugar
1/2 tablespoons salt
1 cup salad oil
1 teaspoon dry mustard

1/3 cup vinegar
2 tablespoons grated yellow onion
1 1/2 teaspoons poppy seeds

In a blender, process all ingredients except poppy seeds until very smooth.

Place ingredients in storage container and add poppy seeds, mixing well to evenly distribute seeds throughout. Store in refrigerator.

Creamy Blue Cheese Dressing

Makes about 1 1/2 cups

1/3 cup crumbled blue cheese
3 tablespoons buttermilk
3 tablespoons sour cream
2 tablespoons mayonnaise
2 teaspoons white wine vinegar

1/4 teaspoon sugar
1/8 teaspoon garlic powder
1/4 teaspoon salt
1/8 teaspoon fresh ground pepper

In a small bowl, mash blue cheese and buttermilk together with a fork until mixture resembles large-curd cottage cheese. Stir in sour cream, mayonnaise, vinegar, sugar, and garlic powder until well-blended. Season to taste with the salt and pepper.

This dreamy dressing takes a wedge salad to the next level.

Roquefort Dressing

Makes about 2 cups

4 ounces blue or Roquefort cheese, crumbled
1/4 cup heavy cream
1/4 cup white wine vinegar
1/2 cup mayonnaise
1/2 teaspoon garlic salt

In a small bowl, combine cheese and cream, mixing well to make a thin paste. Stir in vinegar and mayonnaise; add garlic salt to taste.

This version of a blue cheese dressing also goes well on a wedge salad.

Green Goddess Dressing

Makes 1 1/2 cups

1 avocado, peeled and seed removed
1 cup mayonnaise
2 tablespoons finely chopped green onions
1 tablespoon lemon juice
1 clove garlic, finely chopped
1/2 teaspoon salt
1/4 teaspoon fresh ground pepper

In a blender, combine all of the ingredients. Process until smooth.
Cover tightly and chill for 24 hours before serving.

Cilantro Lime Dressing

Makes about 1 1/2 cups

1 jalapeño pepper, stem removed, seeded, and coarsely chopped

1 clove garlic, finely chopped

3/4 teaspoon finely chopped fresh ginger root

1/4 cup fresh lime juice

1/3 cup honey

2 tablespoons balsamic vinegar

1/2 teaspoon salt

1/4 cup packed cilantro leaves

1/2 cup olive oil

Place the jalapeño pepper, garlic, and ginger into a food processor; pulse until jalapeño and garlic are finely chopped. Add the lime juice, honey, balsamic vinegar, salt, and cilantro; pulse a few times to blend.

With motor running, slowly add olive oil, processing until well-blended and olive oil is incorporated into the dressing. Adjust seasoning to taste.

Italian Salad Dressing

Makes about 1 1/4 cups

3/4 cup vegetable oil
1/4 cup cider vinegar
2 tablespoons water
2 cloves garlic, finely chopped

2 teaspoons sugar
1 1/2 teaspoons salt
1/4 teaspoon fresh ground pepper
1 teaspoon grated Parmesan cheese

In a jar with tight-fitting lid, combine all ingredients. Shake well to combine.

Allow flavors to blend an hour or longer. Store in refrigerator.

Buttermilk Dressing

Makes about 2 cups

1/2 cup sour cream
1/2 cup mayonnaise
2 tablespoons chopped fresh dill
2 tablespoons apple cider vinegar

2 cloves garlic, finely chopped
1 cup buttermilk
1 teaspoon salt
1 teaspoon fresh ground pepper

In a small bowl, stir together sour cream, mayonnaise, dill, vinegar, and garlic. Whisk in buttermilk and season with salt and pepper.

Cover tightly and refrigerate.

This is a standby at our house: always good.

BARBECUE SAUCE

Makes one 16-ounce jar

3 cups ketchup

1/2 cup packed brown sugar

1/2 cup molasses

1/4 cup yellow mustard

2 tablespoons vinegar

2 tablespoons liquid smoke

2 tablespoons Worcestershire sauce

1/2 teaspoon garlic salt

1/4 teaspoon ground white pepper

In a medium saucepan over medium-high heat, mix all ingredients together. Heat until warm throughout. Store in the refrigerator.

BEER MARINADE

Makes about 2 cups

1 12-ounce can beer

1/3 cup peanut oil

1/2 cup finely chopped red onion

2 cloves garlic, finely chopped

3 tablespoons honey

1 tablespoon dried parsley

1 tablespoon dried basil

1/2 teaspoon salt

1/2 teaspoon fresh ground pepper

Stir ingredients together, mixing well.

To marinate steaks, place marinade in a flat dish large enough to hold steaks. Pierce meat with fork and place in dish with marinade. Turn to coat both sides. Cover tightly and refrigerate 12 hours or overnight.

This marinade adds great flavor to round, flank, or New York strip steaks.

Amber's Texas-Style Steak Marinade

Makes about 1 cup

1/2 cup barbecue sauce (see page 98)
1/4 cup ketchup
2 tablespoons Worcestershire sauce
2 teaspoons hot pepper sauce

1 teaspoon lemon juice
1 teaspoon soy sauce
1 teaspoon seasoning salt

Combine ingredients in a large resealable plastic bag.

To marinate steaks, rinse four steaks, rib eye or New York strip, and pat dry. Place steaks in bag with marinade, carefully press out air, and seal. Gently knead the marinade into steaks. Let stand for at least an hour on each side.

Western-Style Steak Sauce

Makes 3 cups

2 cups ketchup
1/2 cup red wine
1/4 cup lemon juice
1/4 cup Worcestershire sauce
1/4 cup finely chopped onion
3 cloves garlic, finely chopped

1 teaspoon chili powder
1/2 teaspoon salt
1/2 teaspoon hot pepper sauce
1 teaspoon horseradish
1/2 cup brown sugar

In a medium saucepan, combine ingredients and cook over medium-low heat. Reduce heat to simmer until desired consistency, about 10 minutes.

Cover tightly and refrigerate.

Spice Steak Rub

Makes rub for four to five steaks

1 teaspoon garlic powder
2 teaspoons ground cumin
2 teaspoons paprika
1 teaspoon chipotle chili powder
1/2 teaspoon fresh ground pepper
1/2 teaspoon salt
1/2 teaspoon ground cinnamon
1 tablespoon olive oil

In a small jar or shaker, combine all dry ingredients.

To use, brush both sides of steak with the olive oil. Sprinkle with spice rub.

New Mexico Herb and Spice Butter

Makes about 1 cup

8 tablespoons butter, softened at room temperature
3 tablespoons finely chopped cilantro
1 clove garlic, finely chopped
1 teaspoon medium-hot Chimayo chili powder
1 teaspoon grated lime peel
1/2 teaspoon ground cumin
1/4 teaspoon dried oregano
1/4 teaspoon salt
1/4 teaspoon fresh ground pepper

In a medium bowl, cream the butter until light and fluffy, using a handheld mixer. On low speed, blend in cilantro, garlic, chili powder, lime zest, cumin, oregano, salt, and pepper. Brush over any type of steak in the last 2 minutes of grilling.

MAPLE-VINEGAR DRIZZLE

Makes 4 to 6 servings

3 tablespoons butter

1/2 cup finely chopped shallots

2/3 cup cider vinegar

1/2 cup maple syrup

In medium saucepan, melt butter over low heat. Add shallots; cook for 5 minutes. Add vinegar and syrup. Cook for 10 minutes over medium-low heat.

This is great drizzled over grilled chicken.

WINE MUSHROOM SAUCE

Makes about 1 1/3 cups

2 tablespoons butter

1 cup sliced fresh mushrooms

1/4 cup finely chopped green onions

1 tablespoon cornstarch

1/2 cup dry red or white wine

2 tablespoons finely chopped parsley

1 teaspoon instant beef bouillon

1/4 teaspoon salt

1/4 teaspoon fresh ground pepper

1 cup water

In a medium saucepan, melt the butter over medium heat. Add mushrooms and onions; cook for 4 to 5 minutes or until tender. Stir in cornstarch. Stir in the wine, parsley, bouillon, salt, pepper, and water. Cook and stir until thickened and bubbly. Cook and stir 1 to 2 minutes more.

Serve this delicious sauce with beef, lamb, veal, or pork.

Perfect Hollandaise Sauce

Makes 6 to 8 servings

3 egg yolks
2 tablespoons lemon juice
4 tablespoons butter, divided use
1/2 cup boiling water
1/2 teaspoon salt
1/2 teaspoon fresh ground pepper
1/8 teaspoon hot red (cayenne) pepper

In a small saucepan, combine egg yolks and lemon juice. Blend until smooth, using a wooden spoon or rubber scraper. Place over low heat; add 2 tablespoons butter. Cook over low heat, stirring constantly, until butter is melted. Add remaining butter and continue stirring until melted.

Add boiling water, a tablespoon at a time, and whisk vigorously to blend. Continue cooking and stirring until sauce is thickened. Remove from heat immediately. Season with salt, pepper, and cayenne.

Sauce may be refrigerated, tightly covered, and reheated in a heavy saucepan over low heat, stirring constantly.

Remoulade Sauce

Makes about 2 cups

3/4 cup mayonnaise
2 tablespoons ketchup
1/2 tablespoon finely chopped green onions
1/2 tablespoon finely chopped fresh parsley
1/2 tablespoon fresh lemon juice
1 tablespoon sweet pickle relish
1/2 teaspoon Creole seasoning
1/2 teaspoon salt
1 tablespoon vinegar
1/2 teaspoon Worcestershire sauce
3 to 4 drops of hot pepper sauce (Tabasco)

In medium bowl, combine all ingredients and mix until well-blended. Cover tightly and refrigerate several hours before serving to allow flavors to blend.

Creamy Horseradish Sauce

Makes about 1 cup

1/2 cup sour cream
2 tablespoons prepared horseradish
1 tablespoon finely chopped green onions
1/4 cup heavy cream (optional)

In a small bowl, combine all ingredients except heavy cream, mixing well. Cover tightly and refrigerate several hours before serving. Chill covered until ready to be served.

If "whipped horseradish cream" is desired, beat heavy cream into soft peaks and blend into sauce just before serving.

This sauce is great for prime rib and roast beef.

Tartar Sauce

Makes 1 cup

1/2 cup mayonnaise

2 tablespoons finely chopped red onion

2 tablespoons finely chopped sweet relish

2 tablespoons Creole mustard

2 teaspoons fresh lime juice

Combine all ingredients in a small bowl, stirring with a whisk. Cover tightly and chill.

Seafood Cocktail Sauce

Makes 1 cup

1/2 cup ketchup

1 tablespoon lemon juice

1 tablespoon prepared horseradish

1 tablespoon Worcestershire sauce

In a small bowl, combine ingredients, mixing well. Cover tightly and refrigerate.

This is the sauce you need for shrimp cocktail.

Chipotle Cream Sauce

Makes about 1 cup

3/4 cup heavy cream
3/4 cup chicken broth
5 tablespoons honey mustard
1 7-ounce can chipotle chilies, drained and finely chopped
1 clove garlic, finely chopped
1/2 teaspoon salt
1 teaspoon fresh lemon juice
1/2 teaspoon fresh ground pepper

In a small saucepan over medium heat, whisk together the cream, broth, honey mustard, chilies, garlic, and salt. Bring to a simmer and cook partially covered, stirring occasionally, until reduced by about 1/3, about 15 minutes. Remove from the heat and stir in the lemon juice and season generously with the pepper. Season with more salt if needed.

Serve warm.

This creamy, spicy sauce is excellent with salmon and shrimp.

Hot Pepper Jelly Dipping Sauce

Makes about 1 1/2 cups

1/2 cup hot and smoky barbecue sauce
1/3 cup orange marmalade
1/3 cup hot pepper jelly
2 tablespoons creamy-style horseradish
1 tablespoon honey mustard
1 tablespoon fresh lime juice

In a medium saucepan over low heat, combine the barbecue sauce, marmalade, jelly, horseradish, honey mustard, and lime juice. Cook, stirring often, just until the jelly has melted.

Serve warm.

Avocado Mayonnaise

Makes 1 1/2 cups

2 large avocados

1/3 cup mayonnaise

1 tablespoon fresh lime juice

3/4 teaspoon hot pepper sauce (Tabasco)

1/2 teaspoon salt

In a small food processor, combine all of the ingredients. Process until smooth, scraping the sides a couple of times.

Creole Mayonnaise

Makes 1/2 cup

4 tablespoons mayonnaise

1 tablespoon Worcestershire sauce

1/2 teaspoon hot pepper sauce (Tabasco)

1 teaspoon Creole seasoning

In a small bowl, combine ingredients and stir well. Cover tightly and refrigerate.

This is so good on sandwiches.

Pizza Sauce

Makes enough sauce for two pizzas

- 1 6-ounce can tomato paste
- 1 cup water
- 2 tablespoons olive oil
- 2 tablespoons butter
- 2 cloves garlic, finely chopped
- 1 tablespoon finely chopped fresh oregano
- 1 tablespoon finely chopped fresh basil
- 1 tablespoon finely chopped fresh parsley
- 1 teaspoon salt
- 1 teaspoon sugar

In a small bowl, blend ingredients to make a smooth sauce. Cover and let stand several hours to blend flavors. Spread over pizza dough and top as desired.

White Cream Gravy

Makes about 3 cups

- 1/3 cup pan drippings from any fried meat or chicken
- 2 tablespoons flour
- 2 cups milk
- Salt and pepper to taste

Remove the steak or chicken from the frying pan, reserving 1/3 cup pan dripping. Over medium heat, stir in flour until smooth and bubbly. Slowly stir in milk, cooking and stirring several minutes to thicken. Season with salt and pepper to taste.

This is the traditional gravy with fried chicken and chicken-fried steak.

Brown Gravy

Makes 3 cups

1 cup turkey or pot roast drippings
2 cups water
4 tablespoons flour
Salt and pepper to taste

Pour drippings into a medium saucepan through a fine mesh strainer to remove any solids. Drippings should be clear. Place saucepan over medium-high heat.

Meanwhile whisk flour into water, stirring until smooth. Heat drippings until boiling; slowly pour in flour mixture, stirring constantly. Add flour gradually to achieve desired thickness; you may not need all of the flour mixture. Turn down the heat and simmer. Add salt and pepper to taste.

Good cooks are always measured by their gravy. This excellent recipe for pot roast or turkey gravy will make sure you measure up.

Breads

TIP

To crush crackers, place them
in a ziplock bag and smash
with a large spoon.

Texas Corn Bread

Makes 6 to 8 servings or 12 muffins

1 cup yellow cornmeal
1/2 cup flour
1 teaspoon salt
(Mix together; then add the ingredients at right without mixing)

1 cup buttermilk
1/2 cup milk
1 egg
1 tablespoon baking powder
1 teaspoon baking soda
1/4 cup butter, melted

Preheat oven to 450 degrees. Grease a 9″ square pan or one muffin pan with a light coat of vegetable oil.

Stir mixture well and pour into pan. Bake for approximately 12-15 minutes.

A very moist corn bread.

Jalapeño Hush Puppies

Makes 30 pieces

2 cups cornmeal
1 tablespoon flour
1/2 teaspoon salt
1 teaspoon baking soda
1 teaspoon baking powder
1 cup buttermilk

1 egg
2 tablespoons finely chopped sweet yellow onion
1/4 cup finely chopped, seeded jalapeño peppers (optional)

Combine all ingredients in medium bowl and mix until smooth. Mixture will be stiff. Drop by tablespoons into a skillet with hot vegetable oil. Cook for 7 to 8 minutes.

Cheddar-Green Onion Muffins

Makes 12 muffins

2 cups flour

1/2 cup cornmeal

1 tablespoon baking powder

1 teaspoon salt

1 teaspoon baking soda

1/2 teaspoon fresh ground pepper

1/2 cup shredded extra-sharp Cheddar cheese, divided

4 tablespoons butter, chilled, cut into pieces

1 1/4 cups buttermilk

2 tablespoons finely chopped green onions

1 clove garlic, finely chopped

1 large egg, lightly beaten

Preheat oven to 375 degrees.

Combine flour, cornmeal, baking powder, baking soda, salt, and pepper in a food processor; pulse three times to combine. Add 5 tablespoons cheese and butter; pulse five times or until mixture resembles coarse crumbs.

In a medium bowl, combine buttermilk, onions, garlic, and egg, stirring with a whisk. Add the flour mixture, stirring just until moist.

Spoon batter into 12 muffin cups sprayed with cooking spray. Sprinkle evenly with remaining 3 tablespoon of cheese. Bake for 18 minutes or until pick test comes out clean. Cool 5 minutes in pan.

Parmesan Garlic Twists

Makes 24 twists

1 package regular breadsticks

1 large egg, lightly beaten

1 1/2 cups finely grated Parmesan cheese

1 tablespoon garlic salt

1 tablespoon poppy or sesame seeds

Heat oven to 400 degrees.

Cut the breadsticks into 24 strips and place them on two baking sheets sprayed with cooking spray. Brush each with egg and sprinkle with cheese, garlic salt, and seeds. Twist the strips and bake until puffed and golden brown, about 12 to 15 minutes.

Cheddar Toasts

Makes 24 to 30 toasts

1 sourdough French bread baguette, sliced 1/8" thick

1 1/2 cups shredded sharp Cheddar cheese

1 teaspoon garlic salt

1/2 teaspoon ground red pepper

1/4 cup butter, melted

Preheat the oven to 375 degrees.

Place baguette slices in a single layer on a baking sheet sprayed with cooking spray; brush each with the butter and flip over. Bake for 7 minutes or until toasted. Turn slices over, coat with cooking spray, sprinkle 1 tablespoon cheese over each slice, and sprinkle with garlic salt. Bake 5 minutes or until cheese melts. Sprinkle with red pepper.

Zucchini Bread

Makes two loaves

- 3 eggs
- 2 cups peeled and grated zucchini
- 1 cup vegetable oil
- 2 cups sugar
- 3 teaspoon vanilla
- 3 cups flour
- 1/2 cup chopped pecans
- 1 teaspoon salt
- 1 teaspoon baking soda
- 1 tablespoon baking powder
- 3 teaspoons cinnamon

Preheat oven to 325 degrees.

Beat eggs until light and foamy. Add oil, sugar, vanilla, and zucchini. Mix lightly but well. Add dry ingredients, mixing well. Mix in nuts.

Grease and flour two loaf pans. Spoon mixture into pans and bake for 1 hour or until done.

Easy Pumpkin Bread

Makes one large or two small loaves

- 1 cup canned pumpkin
- 1 cup sugar
- 3/4 cup cooking oil
- 2 eggs, beaten
- 1 1/2 cups flour
- 1 teaspoon soda
- 1 teaspoon baking powder
- 1 teaspoon nutmeg
- 1 teaspoon cinnamon
- 1/4 teaspoon salt
- 1 teaspoon brown sugar

Preheat oven to 350 degrees.

In a medium bowl, mix all of the dry ingredients. Add the wet ingredients and blend well. Sprinkle top of loaf with the brown sugar; bake for 50 minutes.

Makes a great holiday treat.

Banana Nut Loaf

Makes two loaves

4 large bananas (very ripe)	1/2 teaspoon salt
1/2 cup vegetable oil	2 teaspoons baking soda
1/3 cup buttermilk	1 teaspoon baking powder
1 cup sugar	1 teaspoon vanilla
2 eggs, beaten	1/2 teaspoon cinnamon
2 cups flour	1/2 cup chopped pecans

Preheat oven to 325 degrees.

Mash bananas to a pulp. Blend together the eggs, buttermilk, oil, and bananas. Add the sugar and vanilla and mix again. Mix dry ingredients together and then add to the banana mixture. Add nuts and mix again.

Pour into two well-greased loaf pans, filling halfway full. Bake until bread shrinks from side of pans, approximately 50 to 55 minutes.

Homestyle Croutons

Makes 3 to 4 cups croutons

1 loaf French bread (day old is best)	2 tablespoons garlic salt
1/2 cup butter	1/2 teaspoon parsley
2 tablespoons olive oil	1 tablespoon basil

Preheat oven to 250 degrees.

Slice and cut bread into cubes and place on cookie sheet.

In a small saucepan, melt butter; add olive oil, spices, and garlic and sauté. Pour over croutons; stirring to coat.

Bake for 45 minutes, stirring every 15 minutes. Croutons should be golden and crisp.

Side Dishes

TIP

A wooden spoon inserted into boiling water keeps the water from boiling over.

Homemade Mashed Potatoes

Makes 8 servings

8 large Yukon Gold or russet potatoes

Water as needed

2 teaspoons salt, divided use

1 cup milk

8 tablespoons butter, softened at room temperature (divided use)

1/2 teaspoon fresh ground pepper

Peel and cube potatoes. Place potatoes in a medium saucepan and add enough water to cover. Add 1 teaspoon salt. Over high heat, bring water to a boil and cook potatoes until easily pierced with a fork, about 20 to 25 minutes.

Remove from heat. Using a potato masher, crush potatoes, mixing in 4 tablespoons butter. With a handheld mixer, beat in remaining butter. Gradually add the milk, salt, and pepper. Beat again until potatoes are smooth, adding more milk, if needed, for desired consistency. Season with remaining salt and pepper.

Au Gratin Potatoes
Makes 6 to 8 servings

8 Yukon Gold potatoes, peeled and sliced thin (divided use)

1/2 cup finely chopped red onion, divided use

8 tablespoons butter, thinly sliced (divided use)

1 teaspoon salt

1/2 teaspoon fresh ground pepper

12 individual slices Velveeta, divided use

White truffle oil to taste

2 cups milk

Preheat oven to 350 degrees. Grease a 9″ x 13″ baking dish.

Layer half the potatoes in prepared baking dish. Sprinkle evenly with half the onion. Place half the butter slices evenly over potatoes and sprinkle half the salt and pepper. Arrange six slices of cheese on top. Sprinkle a few drops of the truffle oil over the cheese. Repeat layers. Pour milk over potatoes.

Bake for 45 to 1 hour. Cover with foil if top gets too brown before liquid cooks down and potatoes are tender when pierced with a fork.

Cheddar Baked Potato Slices

Makes 6 to 8 servings

1 10.5-ounce can cream of mushroom soup
1/2 teaspoon paprika
2 teaspoons finely chopped green onions
1/2 teaspoon salt
1/2 teaspoon fresh ground pepper
4 medium russet potatoes, sliced 1/4" thick
1 cup grated Cheddar cheese

Preheat oven to 400 degrees. Grease a 2-quart oblong baking dish.

In small bowl, combine soup, paprika, green onions, salt, and pepper. Arrange potatoes in overlapping rows in bottom of dish. Sprinkle with cheese. Spoon soup mixture over cheese.

Cover with foil; bake for 45 minutes. Uncover and bake an additional 10 minutes or until potatoes are easily pierced with a fork.

Ranch Fries

Makes 6 servings

1 1/2 pounds russet potatoes, rinsed and unpeeled
1 tablespoon olive oil
1 1-ounce package Hidden Valley Ranch Salad Dressing and Seasoning Mix

Preheat oven to 400 degrees. Lightly coat a sheet pan with cooking spray.

Cut potatoes into wedges by cutting lengthwise in half and then slicing each half into three long slices. Brush olive oil over potato wedges. In a large resealable plastic bag, combine potatoes and the salad dressing mix, shaking to coat potatoes evenly.

Place potatoes in a single layer on prepared sheet pan. Lightly coat potatoes with cooking spray. Bake for 20 minutes and turn potatoes. Spray again with cooking spray. Cook for 10 to 20 minutes longer or until potatoes are golden brown and crisp.

Twice-Baked Potatoes

Makes 8 servings

4 large russet potatoes, washed and wrapped in foil
8 tablespoons butter
1 cup milk or as needed
1/4 cup sour cream
8 slices bacon, cooked crisp, drained on paper towels, and crumbled
1 green onion, sliced thin
8 American cheese sliced singles
1 teaspoon salt
1/2 teaspoon fresh ground pepper

Preheat oven to 450 degrees. Place potatoes in oven and bake for 1 hour or until potatoes are soft to the touch, using a hot pad or oven mitt.

Cut potatoes in half. Scoop potato into medium bowl. Reserve potato skin shells. Mash potatoes and butter with a masher or combine with handheld mixer.

Using mixer, combine sour cream and milk, beating at high speed until smooth. Using spoon or spatula, fold in bacon and onions. Add salt and pepper to taste.

Scoop potato mixture back into potato shells or 8 ramekins and top each with slice of American cheese.

Reduce oven temperature to 300 degrees. Bake for approximately 10 to 15 minutes or until cheese has melted and potatoes are warm throughout.

Sweet Potato Crunch

Makes 6 to 8 servings

6 medium sweet potatoes, peeled and cubed

1 cup sugar

1 teaspoon salt

4 eggs, beaten

1/2 cup butter plus 6 tablespoons, divided use

1 cup milk

1 teaspoon vanilla

2/3 cup brown sugar

2/3 cup flour

1 cup pecans

6 tablespoons butter

In a large saucepan, place potatoes in enough cold water to cover. Bring to a boil over high heat and cook until easily pierced with a fork, 20 to 30 minutes.

Preheat oven to 350 degrees. Grease a 9″ x 13″ glass baking dish.

Using a handheld mixer on low speed, beat together cooked sweet potatoes, 1 cup sugar, salt, eggs, 1/2 cup butter, milk, and vanilla until smooth. Place potato mixture into prepared baking dish.

In a microwave-safe bowl, melt remaining 6 tablespoons butter on high for 20 seconds. Stir in brown sugar; then add flour and nuts. Mix well and spread evenly over mashed sweet potato mixture.

Bake for 35 to 40 minutes.

Southern Comfort Sweet Potatoes

Makes 6 to 8 servings

4 pounds sweet potatoes, peeled
1/2 cup butter
1/4 cup Southern Comfort liqueur
1/3 cup orange juice
1/4 cup firmly packed brown sugar
1/8 teaspoon nutmeg
1/8 teaspoon ground cloves
1 teaspoon salt
1/2 cup chopped pecans
1 tablespoon shredded orange peel

Preheat oven to 350 degrees. Coat a 1 1/2-quart baking dish with butter.

In large saucepan, place peeled potatoes in enough water to cover. Bring to a boil over high heat, lower heat to simmer, and cook 35 minutes or until potatoes are easily pierced with a fork. Drain and cool enough to handle; peel.

Return potatoes to saucepan and, using potato masher or handheld mixer, mash potatoes with butter. Add Southern Comfort, orange juice, sugar, and spices.

Place potato mixture into prepared baking dish. Top with nuts and orange rind. Bake for 20 to 30 minute or until bubbly.

This is a great holiday dish.

Grandma Lane's Fried Corn

Makes 4 to 6 servings

8 ears fresh corn, husks and silk removed
8 tablespoons butter
1 teaspoon salt
1/2 teaspoon fresh ground pepper

Using a sharp knife and cutting board, scrape kernels off the ears of corn; place corn in a medium bowl. Then scrape the cobs with a knife to strip the "milk" (creamy white juice) into the bowl.

In a large skillet, melt the butter over low heat. Add the corn and juices, stirring occasionally for 10 minutes. Season with salt and pepper.

Use an iron skillet for this recipe if you're lucky enough to have one.

Creamed Corn

Makes 4 to 6 servings

2 tablespoons butter
2 tablespoons flour
1/2 teaspoon salt
1 1/2 cups heavy whipping cream
1/2 teaspoon fresh ground pepper
2 tablespoons sugar
3 cups frozen whole kernel corn or kernels cut from four ears fresh corn (see previous recipe to prepare fresh corn)

In a heavy saucepan, melt butter over medium heat. Gradually stir in flour and salt, blending until smooth and bubbly. Slowly whisk in heavy whipping cream, stirring until thickened. Add sugar and corn. Lower heat and simmer just until corn is tender, about 5 minutes.

Corn Soufflé

Makes 6 to 8 servings

6 ears fresh corn, cut off the cob

2 15-ounce cans cream-style corn

6 tablespoons butter, melted

1 egg

1/2 teaspoon salt

1/2 teaspoon fresh ground pepper

2 tablespoons milk

1 8.5-ounce box "Jiffy" corn muffin mix

2 tablespoons sour cream

Preheat oven to 350 degrees. Grease a 9″ square baking dish.

Using a sharp knife and cutting board, scrape kernels off the ears of corn; place corn in a medium bowl. Add canned cream-style corn and butter, mixing well.

Beat together the egg, milk, salt, and pepper; stir into corn mixture. Blend in corn muffin mix and sour cream, mixing well.

Pour into prepared baking dish. Bake for 40 to 45 minutes or until firm and golden on top.

You may also pour batter into 6 to 8 greased ramekins for individual servings. Do not fill to the top as mixture will rise while baking.

Corn Bread Stuffing

Makes 10 to 12 servings

2 batches Texas Corn Bread (see page 111)

6 tablespoons butter

4 celery stalks, finely chopped

1/2 onion, finely chopped

2 large 49-ounce cans or 48-ounce containers chicken broth

1 teaspoon salt

1/2 teaspoon fresh ground pepper

2 tablespoons chopped parsley

1 tablespoon rubbed sage

4 eggs, beaten

1/2 cup milk

Preheat oven to 325 degrees. Grease bottom and sides of 9″ x 13″ baking dish or pan.

In large bowl, crumble corn bread.

In a medium skillet over medium-high heat, melt butter. Stir in onion and celery; cook for 2 to 3 minutes or until tender. Add cooked vegetables to corn bread.

Stir broth, salt, pepper, parsley, and sage into corn bread mixture. Beat together the eggs and milk; add to corn bread mixture.

Toss well, using hands if needed, to break up any large chunks of bread. Pack mixture into prepared baking dish. Bake for 50 to 60 minutes. Cover with foil if top begins to brown too much.

Save time and effort when making this recipe by using a food processor to chop onion and celery at the same time. Dressing can be assembled the night before, tightly covered, and refrigerated until ready to bake. This is really helpful during busy holidays.

Honey Rum Carrots

Makes 5 to 6 servings

4 tablespoons butter

4 tablespoons dark rum

1 pound carrots, peeled and sliced 1/2" thick

1 cup water

4 tablespoons honey

1/3 cup dark brown sugar, packed

1 teaspoon salt

1/2 teaspoon pepper

In medium skillet, melt the butter over low heat. Carefully pour in the rum. Add remaining ingredients. Cook over medium-high heat, stirring occasionally, 10 to 15 minutes or until the carrots are tender and the liquid is reduced to a glaze. Adjust seasoning with salt and pepper.

This is an amazing side dish; so good.

Acorn Squash

Makes 2 servings

1 acorn squash, halved and seeded
2 tablespoons butter
4 tablespoons brown sugar

Preheat oven to 350 degrees. Coat a sheet pan with cooking spray.

Place each acorn half upside down on prepared sheet pan. Bake until soft when pierced with a fork, 30 to 45 minutes, depending on size of pieces.

Remove squash from the oven and turn over or, if desired, transfer to a smaller baking dish with higher sides so squash will not slide around too much. Coat fresh dish, if using, with cooking spray before adding squash.

Place 1 tablespoon of butter and 2 tablespoons brown sugar in center of each squash half, stirring to mix. Return squash to oven and bake another 30 minutes, basting edges of squash with butter mixture several times.

This squash is great for a dinner party, as it is easy to make but looks impressive. Increase proportions as needed for more than two servings.

Squash Stir-Fry

Makes 6 to 8 servings

1 tablespoon butter

1 tablespoon olive oil

2 medium yellow squash, sliced

2 medium zucchini, sliced

1/2 pound (8 ounces) cut baby carrots

1 medium red onion, thickly sliced

2 cloves garlic, finely chopped

1 teaspoon salt

1 teaspoon fresh ground pepper

1/2 teaspoon Cavender's All-Purpose Greek Seasoning

2 0.49-ounce packets concentrated chicken broth

1/2 cup chicken broth

In a medium skillet over medium-high heat, combine the butter and olive oil. Add the yellow squash, zucchini, carrots, onion, garlic, Cavender's, salt, and pepper. Cook and stir until vegetables are tender crisp, about 15 to 20 minutes. Stir the concentrated broth and regular broth in and cook until bubbly.

SUMMER SQUASH CASSEROLE

Makes 8 to 10 servings

2 tablespoons olive oil

1 tablespoon butter

2 medium yellow squash, coarsely chopped

2 large zucchini, coarsely chopped

1/2 cup finely chopped onion

1 clove garlic, finely chopped

1 10.5-ounce can cream of mushroom soup

1/2 cup sour cream

1/2 teaspoon salt

1/2 teaspoon fresh ground pepper

1 cup crushed Ritz crackers, about 25

1 tablespoon butter, melted

Preheat oven to 350 degrees. Coat 11" x 7" baking dish with cooking spray.

In a large skillet over medium heat, combine the oil and butter. Add the squash, zucchini, onion, and garlic; cook until tender.

In a large bowl, combine the vegetable mixture, soup, and sour cream. Transfer to prepared baking dish. Combine cracker crumbs and the butter. Sprinkle on top.

Bake uncovered for 25 to 30 minutes or until bubbly.

CREAMED SPINACH

Makes 4 to 6 servings

2 10-ounce packages frozen chopped spinach, thawed and drained
1/2 cup bacon, cooked crisp and crumbled
2 tablespoons finely chopped onion
2 cloves garlic, finely chopped
2 tablespoons flour
1/2 teaspoon salt
1 teaspoon Lawry's seasoned salt
1/2 teaspoon fresh ground pepper
2 cups milk
1 8-ounce package cream cheese, cut into 6 to 8 pieces, softened at room temperature

Drain spinach well and squeeze out excess moisture with hands; chop finely and set aside.

In a heavy skillet, fry bacon until crisp; drain and chop. Set aside.

In reserved bacon drippings, combine the onion and garlic and sauté; stir in flour. Add seasonings and blend thoroughly. Slowly add milk, stirring constantly until thickened. Stir in cream cheese, mixing until smooth. Add spinach and bacon; heat through.

BAKED TOMATOES

Makes 4 servings

4 large ripe beefsteak or East Texas tomatoes, tops cut off
1/4 cup finely grated Romano cheese
1/2 cup seasoned bread crumbs
1/2 tablespoon dried parsley
1/2 teaspoon dried oregano
1 teaspoon garlic salt
1/2 teaspoon fresh ground pepper
2 tablespoons olive oil

Preheat oven to 400 degrees. Coat a 9″ square shallow baking dish with cooking spray.

Place tomatoes, cut ends up, close together in prepared dish.

In a small bowl, combine cheese, bread crumbs, parsley, oregano, garlic salt, and pepper. Sprinkle evenly over tomatoes. Drizzle with the olive oil.

Bake for 20 minutes or until cheese is lightly toasted.

In season, ripe East Texas-grown tomatoes are THE best.

Green Bean Casserole

Makes 5 to 6 servings

2 14.5-ounce cans cut green beans, drained
1 10.5-ounce can cream of mushroom soup
1/2 cup milk
1/2 cup French fried onions, reserving 1 tablespoon
1 teaspoon salt
1/2 teaspoon fresh ground pepper

Preheat oven to 350 degrees. Coat 1 1/2-quart baking dish with cooking spray.

In prepared dish, combine all ingredients, mixing well.

Bake for 25 to 30 minutes or until bubbly. Stir, then sprinkle with reserved French fried onions, and cook for 5 more minutes.

Sautéed Green Beans

Makes 6 to 8 servings

2 pounds fresh green beans, ends trimmed
1 red bell pepper, seeded and sliced thin
1/2 cup thinly sliced red onion
2 tablespoons olive oil
2 tablespoons butter
2 cloves garlic, finely chopped
1 teaspoon Cajun seasoning blend

In a large saucepan over high heat, cover green beans with salted water. Bring to a boil and cook for 10 minutes or until tender-crisp. Drain and plunge into ice water to stop cooking; drain again.

In a large skillet over medium heat, combine the olive oil and butter. Stir in the sliced peppers and onion; cook for 2 minutes. Add garlic and cook 2 more minutes. Stir in green beans. Season to taste with Cajun seasoning and cook, stirring occasionally, until mixture is heated through.

Frijoles Rancheros Beans

Makes 6 to 8 servings

8 ounces uncooked chorizo, casings removed

2 tablespoons vegetable oil

2 medium fresh poblano chili peppers, stems removed, seeded, and finely chopped

1/2 cup finely chopped yellow onion

2 cloves garlic, finely chopped

2 15-ounce cans pinto beans, rinsed and drained (divided use)

2 medium tomatoes, chopped

1 cup chicken broth

1/4 cup chopped fresh cilantro

1/2 teaspoon salt

3 tablespoons lime juice

Grated cheese to taste, if desired

In a large skillet over medium heat, cook chorizo until cooked through and no longer pink, breaking up the sausage while it cooks. Remove chorizo from skillet; drain on paper towels. Add oil to skillet along with chili peppers, onion, and garlic. Cook and stir for 4 to 5 minutes or until tender; set aside.

Place 1 can of drained beans in a bowl. Using a potato masher, mash the beans. Add mashed beans and whole beans to skillet; return to medium heat. Stir in tomatoes, broth, cilantro, and salt. Bring to a boil; reduce heat and simmer, uncovered, for 15 minutes or until slightly thickened, stirring occasionally. Remove from heat and stir in lime juice. If desired, top with cheese.

These delicious beans may be served as a side dish or with tortillas as a dip.

BAKED BEANS

Makes 6 to 8 servings

2 15-ounce cans pork and beans

2 tablespoons finely chopped red onion

1 tablespoon Worcestershire sauce

1 tablespoon yellow mustard

4 tablespoon ketchup

1/4 cup packed brown sugar

Preheat oven to 350 degrees. In a 1 1/2-quart baking dish, combine ingredients, mixing well.

Bake 30 to 45 minutes or until bubbly.

**Served warm or at room temperature,
baked beans are traditional for barbecues or picnics.**

New Year's Southern-Style Black-Eyed Peas

Makes 8 to 10 servings

10 slices bacon, coarsely chopped

1 cup finely chopped onions

1/2 cup finely chopped green bell pepper

1/2 cup finely chopped celery

2 cloves garlic, finely chopped

1 quart hot water

2 cups chicken broth

1 pound dried black-eyed peas, rinsed

1 or 2 jalapeño chili peppers, stems, ribs, and seeds removed, then finely chopped

1/2 teaspoon salt

1/2 teaspoon fresh ground pepper

1/4 teaspoon Cajun seasoning blend

2 bay leaves

4 cups cooked white rice

In a tall stockpot over medium heat, cook the bacon until done but not crisp; add the onion, bell pepper, and celery. Cook until tender. Add the garlic and cook another minute. Add the peas, hot water, and chicken broth; bring to a full boil.

Add the remaining ingredients, reduce heat to medium, and simmer partially covered. Cook for about 80 to 90 minutes or until the peas are tender and creamy. Add extra water or broth to thin if needed. Serve over cooked white rice.

For good luck during the coming year, eat black-eyed peas on New Year's Eve or Day.

NEW ORLEANS RED BEANS AND RICE
Makes 6 to 8 servings

6 slices bacon, cooked crisp and crumbled (reserve drippings)

2 tablespoons finely chopped green onions

2 tablespoons finely chopped red onion

2 tablespoons finely chopped green pepper

1 jalapeño pepper, stem removed, seeded, and finely chopped

2 tablespoons finely chopped celery

1 tablespoon finely chopped fresh parsley

2 cloves garlic, finely chopped

1/2 pound Polish sausage, sliced 1/4" thick

2 15-ounce cans kidney beans, drained and rinsed

1 cup chicken broth

1 6-ounce can tomato paste

1 teaspoon Gebhardt chili powder

1 tablespoon Worcestershire sauce

1 teaspoon salt

1/2 teaspoon fresh ground pepper

1/2 teaspoon ground red (cayenne) pepper

1/2 teaspoon paprika

2 whole bay leaves

1 teaspoon dried thyme

4 cups cooked white rice

Additional chopped parsley for garnish

In a large Dutch oven or stockpot over medium-high heat, cook the bacon until crisp. Remove from pan using a slotted spoon and drain on paper towels. To the drippings, add onions, peppers, celery, parsley, and garlic; cook until softened, about 5 minutes.

Stir in bacon, sausage, and beans. Add remaining ingredients. Reduce heat and simmer for about an hour. Serve over cooked rice and garnish with parsley.

Side Dishes

Pasta and Rice

TIP

Put a teaspoon of vegetable oil in the water for boiling pasta so the pasta does not stick together.

Bow Tie Pasta with Marinara Sauce

Makes 6 to 8 servings

2 tablespoons butter

2 tablespoons olive oil

1/4 cup finely chopped green onions

2 cloves garlic, finely chopped

2 14.5-ounce cans chopped tomatoes, undrained

1 tablespoons lemon juice

1 teaspoon oregano

1 teaspoon basil

1 teaspoon parsley

2 bay leaves

1 teaspoon salt

1/2 teaspoon fresh ground pepper

1 tablespoon sugar

8 ounces bow tie pasta, cooked according to package directions

1/4 cup Parmesan cheese

In large saucepan over medium-high heat, combine olive oil and butter. Add onion and garlic, stirring constantly and scraping brown bits, until vegetables are tender and golden, about 5 to 7 minutes.

Stir in tomatoes and remaining ingredients except pasta and cheese. Bring to a boil; reduce heat to medium and cook, stirring occasionally, 20 minutes or until most of the liquid evaporates. Remove from heat; discard bay leaves.

Toss the bow tie pasta with 2 cups of marinara sauce. Sprinkle with Parmesan cheese.

Fettuccine Alfredo

Makes 4 to 6 servings

1 8-ounce package fettuccine
4 tablespoons butter
2 cloves garlic, finely chopped
1 cup chicken broth
1 teaspoon salt
1/2 teaspoon fresh ground pepper
1 cup heavy cream
1/2 cup grated Parmesan cheese
1 teaspoon chopped parsley

Cook pasta according to package directions.

Meanwhile, in a medium saucepan, melt butter over low heat. Add garlic, broth, salt, and pepper, mixing well. Add cream, stirring to combine.

When pasta is almost done, lift out with tongs, draining excess water, and blend into sauce. Turn up heat to medium and stir together. Add cheese and stir again. Adjust seasoning and garnish with parsley.

Macaroni and Cheese

Makes 6 to 8 servings

1 12-ounce package elbow macaroni, cooked according to package directions
1 cup milk
4 tablespoons butter, cut in four pieces
8 ounces Velveeta cheese, cubed
1 teaspoon salt
1/2 teaspoon pepper

Preheat oven to 350 degrees. Coat a 1 1/2-quart baking dish with cooking spray.

In prepared baking dish, combine cooked macaroni with remaining ingredients, stirring to mix well.

Bake 20 to 25 minutes, stirring occasionally or until bubbly and brown at the edges.

New Mexico Green Chili Macaroni and Cheese

Makes 4 servings

1 12-ounce package elbow macaroni, cooked according to package directions
4 tablespoons butter
4 tablespoons flour
2 cups whole milk
1 teaspoon salt
1/2 teaspoon fresh ground pepper
2 cups grated Gruyère cheese
1/2 cup chopped green chili
4 tablespoons plain bread crumbs

Preheat oven to 300 degrees. Coat a 1 1/2-quart baking dish or four 1-cup ramekins with cooking spray. Cover a cookie sheet with foil.

Drain cooked macaroni and reserve.

In a large saucepan over medium to low heat, melt the butter. Add the flour, stirring to blend. Slowly add the milk, stirring with a wood spoon. Keep stirring until mixture thickens. Add the salt and pepper and taste.

Turn down the heat to low and add the cheese, green chili, and pasta. Simmer and stir for about a minute.

Pour the mixture into prepared baking dish or ramekins. Place dishes on a foil-wrapped cookie sheet. Lightly cover baking dish or dishes with foil and bake for 10 minutes, just to heat through.

Remove foil covering, top with the bread crumbs, and set the oven to broil. Slide the baking sheet back under the broiler for a minute or two or until bread crumbs are lightly browned. Serve immediately.

This is one of my dinner party favorites.

Spaghetti with Garlic, Olive Oil, and Chili Pepper

Makes 4 to 6 servings

1 16-ounce package thin spaghetti, cooked according to package directions

1/2 cup olive oil

2 cloves garlic, finely chopped

1 medium fresh red or green hot chili pepper, stem removed, seeded, and finely chopped

1 teaspoon salt

1/2 teaspoon fresh ground red (cayenne) pepper

1/2 cup finely chopped fresh flat-leaf parsley

Drain pasta and reserve in large serving bowl. Also reserve 1/2 cup pasta cooking liquid.

In a medium skillet, combine oil, garlic, chili pepper, salt, and ground red pepper; heat over medium heat until oil begins to bubble, about 2 minutes. Add parsley and reserved pasta cooking liquid; stir to combine.

Remove from heat. Pour over pasta and mix well to combine.

BROCCOLI-RICE CASSEROLE

Makes 6 to 8 servings

1 10-ounce package frozen chopped broccoli, cooked and drained

2 tablespoons butter

2 tablespoons finely chopped onion

2 cups cooked rice

1 10.5-ounce can cream of mushroom soup

1 15-ounce jar Cheez Whiz

1 teaspoon salt

1/2 teaspoon fresh ground pepper

Preheat oven to 350 degrees. Coat a 1 1/2-quart baking dish with cooking spray.

Place broccoli in prepared dish. In a small skillet over medium-high heat, combine butter and onions. Cook 2 to 3 minutes or until onion softens. Add onion to broccoli along with rice, soup, and Cheez Whiz, stirring well.

Bake for 45 to 50 minutes.

SPANISH RICE

Makes 6 to 8 servings

2 tablespoons butter

1 cup uncooked rice

2 teaspoons finely chopped onion

1 clove garlic, finely chopped

1 tablespoon chopped green chili peppers

1 teaspoon salt

1 tablespoon chili powder

1/2 teaspoon ground cumin

1 teaspoon chopped fresh cilantro

1 14.5-ounce can chopped tomatoes, undrained

1 1/2 cups water

In a large skillet over medium-high heat, melt the butter; add rice and onion. Stir occasionally and cook until light brown. Add garlic and green chili peppers; cook 2 to 3 minutes longer. Stir in salt, tomatoes with the juice, 1 1/2 cups water, chili powder, cumin, and cilantro. Bring mixture to a boil. Reduce heat to low, cover and simmer for 15 to 20 minutes or until all the water is absorbed and rice is tender.

Fried Rice

Makes 6 to 8 servings

2 cups uncooked rice

6 tablespoons butter

2 eggs, beaten

1/2 cup milk

1/2 teaspoon salt

1/4 teaspoon fresh ground pepper

2 carrots, peeled and chopped

2 green onions, finely chopped

1/2 cup soy sauce

Cook rice according to package directions; reserve.

In a large skillet over medium heat, melt the butter.

In a small bowl, beat the eggs with the milk and salt and pepper. Add to butter, stirring and cooking until eggs are set. Add the carrots and onions, mixing well. Gradually add rice and the soy sauce, stirring constantly until thoroughly combined.

Serve immediately.

Main Dishes

Beef

Make some dishes family traditions.

Momma's Meatloaf

Makes 6 to 8 servings

1 1/2 pounds ground round beef

*1 15-ounce can whole peeled tomatoes,
    drained and chopped, juice reserved*

1 15-ounce can tomato sauce

3 tablespoons Worcestershire sauce

1/3 cup finely chopped green bell pepper

1/3 cup finely chopped yellow onion

1 teaspoon garlic salt

1/2 teaspoon fresh ground pepper

2 eggs, beaten

1/4 cup milk

*20 saltine crackers, crushed fine in blender,
    food processor, or resealable plastic bag*

*8 individual slices American cheese,
    unwrapped, stacked, and cut into small cubes*

Preheat oven to 350 degrees. Coat a 9″ square baking dish with cooking spray.

In a medium bowl, combine the meat, crushed tomatoes, Worcestershire sauce, bell pepper, onion, garlic salt, and pepper; mix well.

Beat eggs with the milk. Add the egg mixture and crushed crackers to the meat mixture, mixing well with clean hands. Mix in cheese. Fold into prepared baking dish, shaping into a "loaf," covering any exposed cheese with the meat.

Bake 30 minutes and then top with tomato sauce and reserved tomato juice. Bake an additional 45 to 50 minutes, spooning sauce over the top every 20 minutes. Let stand 10 minutes and slice.

Crock-Pot Pot Roast

Makes 6 to 8 servings

2 tablespoons vegetable oil

6 to 8 pounds beef rump or eye-of-round roast

1 tablespoon garlic salt

1 tablespoon fresh ground pepper

4 large Yukon Gold potatoes, peeled and cubed

8 carrots, peeled and sliced

1 2-ounce package Lipton Onion Soup and Dip Mix

1 2-ounce package Lipton Beefy Mushroom Soup Mix

1 10.5-ounce can cream of mushroom soup

1 14-ounce can beef broth

In large Dutch oven over medium heat, warm the oil, add roast, and cook on all sides until brown. Season meat with garlic salt and pepper.

Turn crock-pot to high setting and arrange potatoes and carrots on the bottom, placing roast on top of vegetables. Using a fine mesh strainer, sift dry soups to eliminate dry onions or sprinkle soup mixes directly onto meat.

Add mushroom soup and broth, stirring to combine. Cook on high for 5 to 6 hours until roast is easily pierced with a fork. Keep warm on low setting.

This recipe makes plenty of delicious brown gravy to serve with the roast.

Smothered Swiss Steak

Makes 4 to 6 servings

1 pound beef round steak, pounded to tenderize and cut into 4 to 6 serving pieces

2 tablespoons vegetable oil

1 teaspoon garlic powder

1 teaspoon salt

1/2 teaspoon fresh ground pepper

1 medium sweet yellow onion, sliced 1/4" thick

2 tablespoons flour

1 28-ounce can whole tomatoes, chopped

1 cup tomato juice

1/2 cup water

2 tablespoons Worcestershire sauce

1/2 cup ketchup

1/2 green bell pepper, seeded and sliced 1/4" thick

Season pieces of meat with the garlic powder, salt, and pepper.

In a large skillet over medium-high heat, warm the oil, add meat, and brown beef about 5 minutes on each side. Remove meat from pan and keep warm.

Add the onion to the pan and cook in pan drippings, stirring in flour while cooking to coat onion. Add tomatoes and tomato juice, water, Worcestershire sauce, ketchup, and bell pepper. Return meat to skillet, pressing meat among vegetables and into sauce.

Simmer over low heat for about an hour or until meat is fork tender.

The gravy make a great sauce over mashed potatoes.

Green Pepper Steak

Makes 5 to 6 servings

1 1/2 pounds round steak, fat trimmed, cut into 1/2" thick strips

1/4 cup flour

1 teaspoon salt

1 teaspoon fresh ground pepper

1/4 cup butter

1/2 cup finely chopped green onions

3 cloves garlic, finely chopped

1 teaspoon oregano

1 1/4 cups water

2 teaspoons beef broth concentrate

2 teaspoons Worcestershire sauce

3 large green peppers, stemmed, seeded, cut into 1/2" strips

2 medium tomatoes, cut into four pieces

1 to 2 tablespoons each, flour and water (optional)

2 cups cooked rice

Coat meat strips in mixture of flour, salt, and pepper.

Melt butter in a large skillet over medium-high heat. Place the meat in the pan and cook until well-browned on all sides. Add onion, garlic, oregano, water, and beef broth concentrate. Cover skillet and simmer for about 1 1/2 hours or until meat is tender.

Remove skillet lid and stir in Worcestershire sauce and add green pepper strips. Cover and simmer for 15 minutes. If thicker consistency is desired, blend in mixture of equal parts flour and cold water, stirred to make a smooth paste. Add tomatoes and heat for 5 minutes longer.

Serve over rice.

Smoky Marinated Beef Brisket

Makes 8 to 10 servings

8–10 pound brisket, fat trimmed
1 tablespoon garlic salt
1 teaspoon freshly ground pepper
1 cup Liquid Smoke
1 cup Worcestershire sauce
Barbecue sauce (see page 98)

Season meat on all sides with garlic salt and pepper. Mix together liquid smoke and Worcestershire sauce and pour over brisket in non-reactive baking dish. Cover with heavy foil and marinate overnight, turning once.

Preheat oven to 225 degrees or ready a charcoal grill or gas smoker. Bake, covered, in the oven or smoke indirectly over low heat for 7 to 8 hours or until very tender.

Slice into thin strips and serve with barbecue sauce.

American Steakhouse-Style Beef

Makes 6 servings

1 1/2 pounds lean boneless top sirloin steak
1/3 cup soy sauce
1/3 cup pineapple juice
1/3 cup dry sherry
1/4 cup cider vinegar

Place steak in large shallow dish.

Combine remaining ingredients and pour over steak. Cover tightly with plastic wrap and chill 4 hours, turning steak occasionally. Drain, discarding marinade.

Grill over hot coals (400 to 500 degrees) 10 minutes on each side or till desired degree of doneness.

To serve, slice across grain into thin slices.

No-Grill Skillet Beef Tenderloin

Makes 4 servings

4 6-ounce beef tenderloin steaks, 1/2" thick

1 teaspoon garlic salt

1/2 teaspoon fresh ground pepper

2 tablespoons butter

2 tablespoons olive oil

4 shallots, finely chopped

3 tablespoons Cognac or brandy

3/4 cup beef broth

1 tablespoon butter, softened at room temperature

1 teaspoon finely chopped fresh parsley

1/2 teaspoon pink peppercorns, crushed

Season steaks on both sides with garlic salt and pepper.

In a large skillet, heat the butter and oil over medium-high heat. Cook steaks 1 to 2 minutes or until brown on one side. Reduce heat to medium and turn steaks. Cook 6 minutes more or until desired doneness. Remove steaks and keep warm.

Add shallots to skillet and cook 5 minutes or until tender. Remove skillet from heat; add Cognac. Return skillet to medium heat; cook for 2 minutes, stirring to scrape up browned bits from pan. Add broth and reduce heat to medium-low. Whisk in 1 tablespoon softened butter until smooth. Return steaks to skillet. Heat, spooning sauce over steaks. Top with parsley and peppercorns.

Slow Cooker Beef Stroganoff

Makes 6 to 8 servings

3 tablespoons butter (1 teaspoon reserved)
3 tablespoons vegetable oil (1 teaspoon reserved)
2 pounds lean boneless top beef sirloin, fat trimmed, sliced into thin strips
3 tablespoons finely chopped green onions
2 cloves garlic, finely chopped
1 teaspoon salt
1 teaspoon fresh ground pepper
1 14-ounce can beef broth
1/2 cup dry vermouth or white wine
3 tablespoons flour
1 teaspoon Worcestershire sauce
1/2 teaspoon ground thyme
1/2 teaspoon paprika
1/2 teaspoon crushed oregano
1/2 teaspoon finely chopped parsley
1 2-ounce package Lipton Onion Soup and Dip Mix
1 2-ounce package Lipton Beefy Mushroom Soup Mix
1 10.5-ounce can cream of mushroom soup
1/2 pound mushrooms, cleaned and sliced
1 cup sour cream
1 16-ounce package wide egg noodles, cooked according to package directions

In a large skillet over medium-high heat, melt the butter and oil. Cook meat for 8 to 10 minutes or until brown. Stir in the green onions, garlic, salt, and pepper. Add the broth and vermouth or wine, stirring to loosen bits from bottom of pan. Transfer meat mixture to the slow cooker.

Stir in flour, Worcestershire sauce, thyme, paprika, oregano, and parsley. Using a fine mesh strainer, sift dry soups to eliminate dry onions or sprinkle soup mixes directly onto meat. Add the mushroom soup and stir until blended.

In a small skillet over medium-high heat, melt reserved 1 teaspoon of the oil and butter. Add mushrooms and cook 1 minute. Stir mushrooms into slow cooker.

Cover and cook on high setting for 3 to 4 hours or until meat is fork tender. Add sour cream and cover and cook until blended. Serve over cooked noodles.

Tequila-Marinated Fajitas

Makes 18 to 20 fajitas; serves 6 to 8

1 cup tequila

1 cup olive oil

2 limes, juiced

2 lemons, juiced

3 cloves garlic, finely chopped

1/4 cup crushed red chili flakes

2 tablespoons salt

2 tablespoons oregano

1 tablespoons fresh ground pepper

5 pounds sirloin steak, thinly sliced

3 bell peppers, stemmed, seeded, and sliced

3 yellow onions, sliced

6 jalapeño peppers, stemmed, seeded, and sliced

Flour tortillas, sour cream, salsa, and guacamole for garnish

Combine the tequila, olive oil, lime juice, lemon juice, garlic, red chili flakes, salt, oregano, and pepper in a large bowl and mix well. Add the steak and toss to coat. Marinate, covered in the refrigerator, for 8 to 10 hours, stirring occasionally.

Drain the steak, discarding the marinade. Heat a large skillet over high heat. Cook the steak strips in several batches, stirring until light brown on all sides; reserve. Add the peppers and onions to skillet, stirring and cooking until the vegetables are tender. Return meat to skillet and heat through.

Serve with warm tortillas to wrap the meat mixture. Garnish with sour cream, salsa, and guacamole.

Mongolian Beef

Makes 4 to 6 servings

2 tablespoons soy sauce

1 teaspoon sugar

1 teaspoon cornstarch

2 teaspoons sherry

2 teaspoons hoisin sauce

1 teaspoon white vinegar

1 teaspoon red chili paste

1/2 teaspoon salt

1/2 teaspoon fresh ground pepper

3 tablespoons vegetable oil, divided use

3 teaspoons olive oil

1 tablespoon finely chopped fresh ginger

1 clove garlic, finely chopped

1 pound sirloin steak, trimmed of fat, thinly sliced across the grain

16 green onions, cleaned and cut into 2" pieces

2 cups cooked rice

In a small bowl, combine soy sauce, sugar, cornstarch, sherry, hoisin sauce, vinegar, chili paste, salt, and 1 tablespoon vegetable oil. Stir until smooth; reserve.

In a large skillet over medium-high heat, warm 2 tablespoons vegetable oil. When oil is hot, stir in ginger, garlic, and beef; cook for 5 to 7 minutes or until beef is browned. Add onions; cook for 30 seconds.

Add reserved soy sauce mixture and cook for 1 minute or until thickened, stirring constantly. Simmer for 3 to 5 minutes to blend flavors.

Serve over rice.

Italian Meatballs

Makes about 30 meatballs; 6 to 8 servings

2 pounds ground beef

1 pound ground pork

2 eggs, beaten

1/2 cup milk

1 cup bread crumbs

1 teaspoon garlic salt

1/2 teaspoon fresh ground pepper

2 tablespoons Worcestershire sauce

1/3 cup finely chopped yellow onion

1 teaspoon dried oregano

1 tablespoon chopped fresh parsley

1/2 cup grated Parmesan cheese

4 tablespoons olive oil, divided use

Spaghetti sauce as desired; see next recipe

In large bowl, combine all ingredients except olive oil, mixing well with clean hands. Shape meatballs about the size of a golf ball.

In large skillet over medium-high heat, warm 2 tablespoons olive oil. Cook half the meatballs, about 20 minutes, turning to brown all sides. Repeat with remaining oil and meatballs.

Serve with favorite spaghetti sauce (see next recipe) and cooked pasta.

Meat Sauce for Spaghetti

Makes 8 to 10 servings

2 pounds lean ground round

2 tablespoons vegetable oil

1/2 cup finely chopped yellow onion

3 cloves fresh garlic, finely chopped

2 teaspoons salt

3 15-ounce cans whole tomatoes, chopped

3 6-ounce cans tomato paste

2 cups water

2 tablespoons parsley

2 tablespoons basil

2 tablespoons oregano

2 bay leaves

1 tablespoon sugar

1 1-pound package spaghetti, cooked according to package directions

In a large stockpot or Dutch oven over medium-high heat, cook meat in vegetable oil until no longer pink. Add onion, garlic, and salt; cook 3 to 5 minutes or until meat is browned. Add remaining ingredients, stirring to mix well. Lower heat and simmer for about 2 hours, stirring often, to get full flavor.

Serve over cooked spaghetti or other pasta.

This sauce can be made omitting the ground beef and used with meatballs in previous recipe.

Lasagna

Makes 8 to 10 servings

16 ounces fresh ricotta cheese

1/2 cup grated Parmesan cheese, divided use

1 tablespoon dried parsley

1 teaspoon salt

1 1/2 teaspoons dried oregano leaves

1 16-ounce box lasagna noodles, cooked according to package directions

1 recipe meat sauce for spaghetti (see previous recipe)

2 cups shredded mozzarella cheese, divided use

Preheat oven to 350 degrees. Spray a 9″ x 13″ baking or lasagna pan with cooking spray.

In a medium bowl, combine ricotta cheese, 1/4 cup Parmesan cheese, parsley, salt, and oregano. In prepared pan, arrange a layer using 1/3 of the cooked noodles and cover with 1/3 of the sauce mixture, 1 cup mozzarella cheese, and 1/2 of the ricotta cheese mixture.

Repeat layer of noodles, sauce, mozzarella, and ricotta mixture. Cover with layer of noodles. Spoon remaining sauce over noodles; sprinkle with remaining 1/4 cup Parmesan cheese.

Bake uncovered for 45 minutes. Let stand 15 minutes before cutting.

Top servings with any extra sauce.

Oven-Baked Chili Spaghetti with Cheese

Makes 5 to 6 servings

2 tablespoons vegetable oil

1 pound lean ground beef

1/4 cup finely chopped yellow onion

1 teaspoon garlic salt

2 tablespoons Gebhardt chili powder

1 16-ounce package thin spaghetti, cooked according to package directions

1 11.5-ounce can tomato juice

1 15-ounce can whole tomatoes, chopped, undrained

1 cup water

10 individual slices American cheese

Preheat oven to 375 degrees. Coat a deep 9" x 13" baking dish with cooking spray.

In a medium skillet, heat the oil over medium-high heat. Add the meat, onion, and garlic salt; cook until brown. Stir in chili powder to coat the meat.

In prepared baking dish, combine meat, tomato juice, tomatoes, and water. Stir in cooked and drained spaghetti. Arrange slices of cheese over top.

Bake for 20 to 25 minutes or until cheese is bubbling but not too browned.

My daddy's favorite.

Easy Beef Tacos

Makes 6 to 8 servings

12 crispy taco shells
2 tablespoons vegetable oil
1 1/2 pounds lean ground beef
1/4 cup finely chopped yellow onion
1 teaspoon garlic salt
2 tablespoons Gebhardt chili powder
1 teaspoon cumin
1 large tomato, chopped
1 cup shredded Cheddar cheese
1 cup shredded lettuce
1/2 cup sour cream, optional

Preheat oven to 300 degrees.

Wrap the taco shells in foil and place in the oven to warm.

In a large skillet, heat the oil over medium heat. Add beef, onion, garlic salt, chili powder, and cumin; stir and cook until meat is no longer pink. Lower heat and simmer for 5 minutes.

Fill warm taco shells with meat. Garnish as desired with chopped tomato, cheese, lettuce, and sour cream.

Mexican Meat Pie

Makes 5 to 6 servings

2 tablespoons vegetable oil

1 1/2 pounds ground sirloin

1/4 cup finely chopped yellow onion

2 cloves garlic, finely chopped

1/4 cup finely chopped green bell pepper

1 tablespoon Gebhardt chili powder

1 1/2 teaspoons cumin

1 28-ounce can whole tomatoes, chopped

1 10-ounce can Rotel diced tomatoes and green chilies

1 15-ounce can whole kernel corn, drained

2 15-ounce cans pinto beans, drained

1 teaspoon garlic salt

1/2 teaspoon fresh ground pepper

12 corn tortillas, cut into 1/4" strips (divided use)

16 wrapped Velveeta slices (1 package), unwrapped

1 10.5-ounce can cream of chicken soup

Preheat oven to 350 degrees.

In a medium skillet, heat the oil over medium-high heat. Add the meat and cook until brown, stirring in onion, garlic, and bell pepper. Stir in chili powder and cumin to coat the meat. Add both cans of tomatoes, corn, beans, salt, and pepper.

In a 9" x 13" baking dish, layer (in order) half the tortilla strips, meat mixture, and cheese. Repeat layers using remaining ingredients. Spread the soup on top.

Bake for 35 to 40 minutes or until bubbly.

Easy Cheesy Beef Enchiladas

Makes 6 to 8 servings

2 tablespoons vegetable oil

1 1/2 pounds lean ground beef

1/4 cup finely chopped yellow onion

1 teaspoon garlic salt

2 tablespoons Gebhardt chili powder

1 teaspoon cumin

1 dozen 10″ flour tortillas,

1 10.5-ounce can cream of chicken soup

1 10-ounce can Rotel diced tomatoes and green chilies

1 16-ounce package Velveeta, cut into cubes

Preheat oven to 350 degrees. Coat a 9″ x 13″ baking dish with cooking spray.

In a large skillet, heat oil over medium heat. Add beef, onion, and garlic salt. Cook until meat is no longer pink, about 3 to 5 minutes. Stir in chili powder and cumin; lower heat and simmer for 5 minutes.

Spread mixture down center of tortillas and roll tightly. Place rolled tortillas seam side down, sides touching, in prepared baking dish.

In a medium saucepan over medium heat, combine remaining ingredients and cook until cheese is melted; spoon evenly over enchiladas, covering ends and sides.

Cover tightly with foil and bake for 15 minutes or until bubbly.

American Chop Suey

Makes 7 to 8 servings

2 tablespoons butter

2 tablespoons olive oil

1/2 cup finely chopped yellow onion

1/2 cup finely chopped green bell pepper

2 cloves garlic, finely chopped

1 pound ground sirloin

1 tablespoon dried oregano

1 tablespoon dried basil

1 teaspoon salt

1/2 teaspoon fresh ground pepper

1 16-ounce can chopped tomatoes, undrained

1 16-ounce can tomato sauce

1 6-ounce can tomato paste

2/3 cup tomato juice

1 teaspoon sugar

1 16-ounce package elbow macaroni, cooked according to package directions

In a large pot over medium heat, melt the butter and the olive oil together. Add the onion and bell pepper and cook, stirring occasionally until tender, about 5 minutes. Stir in garlic and cook for another minute. Stir in ground sirloin and cook, stirring to break the meat into smaller pieces. Cook about 7 to 8 minutes or until the meat is no longer pink.

Stir in the spices, salt, and pepper. Add the tomatoes with the juice, tomato sauce, tomato paste, and tomato juice. Add sugar. Reduce heat to medium-low and simmer for 15 to 20 minutes. Stir cooked and drained macaroni into the skillet.

Serve immediately.

Main Dishes

Poultry

TIP

Flower arrangements look better and cleaner when the leaves are torn off the stems before putting them in a vase.

Sour Cream Chicken

Makes 5 to 6 servings

6 chicken breast halves, boneless and skinless

6 tablespoons butter

3 cloves garlic, finely chopped

1 teaspoon salt

1 teaspoon fresh ground pepper

1 whole yellow onion, sliced into thin strips

1 cup white wine

1 cup sour cream

Trim fat off chicken and cut each breast half into three to four pieces.

In a large skillet over medium-high heat, melt the butter; add the chicken. Cook until brown on all sides, about 4 to 5 minutes. Add garlic, salt, and pepper; stir into chicken. Add onion and stir again.

Pour in wine, reduce heat, and simmer, covered, for 1 hour. When chicken is tender, add sour cream and serve when mixture is blended and hot throughout. Do not allow to boil.

Serve with mashed potatoes.

This is another Hensel family favorite.

CHICKEN SPAGHETTI

Makes 6 to 8 servings

6 chicken breasts, skinless and boneless
6 cups water
2 14-ounce cans chicken broth, divided use
2 stalks fresh celery, trimmed and cut into two pieces
2 tablespoons butter
1 teaspoon salt
1/2 teaspoon fresh ground pepper

1 16-ounce package spaghetti
1 10.5-ounce can cream of chicken soup
1 10.5-ounce can cream of mushroom soup
1 10.5-ounce can cream of celery soup
1 16-ounce package Velveeta cheese, cut into bite-size pieces.

Preheat oven to 350 degrees. Coat a 9″ x 13″ baking dish with cooking spray.

In large saucepan over medium-high heat, combine chicken, water, 1 can chicken broth, celery stalks, butter, salt, and pepper. Bring to a boil; lower heat and simmer until cooked through, about 20 minutes.

Remove chicken from the broth and cut into bite-size pieces.

Using a colander or fine mesh strainer, pour broth through to remove solids. Return strained broth to saucepan and add remaining can of broth; bring to boil. Stir spaghetti into boiling broth and cook for about 8 to 10 minutes, or until al dente.

Reduce heat to medium. Blend in remaining soups, cut-up chicken, and cheese, stirring often until cheese is melted.

Pour this mixture into prepared baking dish. Bake for 25 to 30 minutes or until bubbly.

This timeless casserole is great for potluck dinners or to take to a friend who's recuperating.

Chicken Cacciatore

Makes 6 servings

6 chicken breast halves, skinless and boneless

2 tablespoons olive oil

1 teaspoon salt

1/2 teaspoon fresh ground pepper

1/2 teaspoon garlic powder

2 tablespoons butter, melted

1 15-ounce can whole tomatoes, chopped

1 cup water

1 6-ounce can tomato paste

1 medium yellow onion, sliced into thin strips

1 tablespoon dried parsley

1 tablespoon dried basil

1 tablespoon dried oregano

1 tablespoon sugar

2 bay leaves

4 cups cooked rice

Preheat oven to 350 degrees. Coat 9″ x 13″ baking dish with cooking spray.

Brush chicken breast halves on both sides with the olive oil; season with the salt, pepper, and garlic powder. Pour melted butter into baking dish, swirl to distribute evenly. Arrange seasoned chicken pieces in single layer in bottom of baking dish.

Bake chicken until browned, turning once, about 10 minutes on each side.

In large bowl, combine tomatoes, water, tomato paste, onion, parsley, basil, oregano, sugar, and bay leaves, mixing well. Pour evenly over chicken. Return to oven for 50 to 60 minutes or until chicken is tender. Remove bay leaves.

Serve over rice.

Classic Chicken Ring

Makes 4 to 5 servings

2 8-ounce packages refrigerated crescent rolls

1/2 cup finely chopped red bell pepper

1/2 cup finely chopped broccoli

1/4 cup finely chopped water chestnuts

2 tablespoons finely chopped yellow onion

1 cup shredded Colby Jack cheese

2 cups cooked, shredded chicken breast

1 10.5-can cream of chicken soup

1 teaspoon salt

1/2 teaspoon fresh ground pepper

Preheat oven to 375 degrees.

Unroll and separate crescent rolls; arrange pointed ends out on greased round pizza stone.

Place all of the vegetables in a food processor; pulse to combine. Move to medium-sized bowl and add remaining ingredients. Stir to combine. Spoon mixture evenly onto center of roll. Fold pointed ends over filling toward the center, leaving a 5″ opening in the middle of the ring. Don't worry if mixture is exposed in places; dough does not have to cover mixture entirely.

Bake for 25 to 30 minutes or until crust is brown and insides are bubbling.

Chicken Pot Pie

Makes 5 to 6 servings

4 chicken breast halves, skinless and boneless, cut into cubes

1 cup carrots, peeled and sliced thin

1 cup frozen peas

2 stalks celery, halved

2 tablespoons plus 1/3 cup butter, divided use

4 cups water

1/2 cup finely chopped celery

1/3 cup finely chopped onion

2 cloves garlic, finely chopped

2 tablespoons flour

1 teaspoon salt

1/2 teaspoon fresh ground pepper

1/4 teaspoon celery seed

1 1/2 cups chicken broth

1 cup milk

2 9" unbaked pie crusts (1 box)

Preheat oven to 425 degrees.

In a medium stockpot over medium-high heat, combine chicken, carrots, peas, celery stalks, 2 tablespoons butter, and water. Boil for 15 minutes. Remove from heat; strain through a strainer; save the broth. Discard celery stalks, reserving remaining chicken and vegetables.

In a medium skillet, melt 1/3 cup butter over medium heat. Add garlic, onion, and chopped celery; sauté until soft but not brown. Stir in flour, salt, pepper, and celery seed. Slowly stir in reserved cooking liquid, 1 1/2 cups chicken broth, and milk. Simmer over medium-low heat until thick. Remove from heat and set aside.

Press one pie crust into the bottom of a 9" ungreased glass pie pan. Place the cooked chicken and vegetables evenly in the bottom of the pie crust. Pour hot mixture over pie crust. Cover with other pie crust, sealing edges. Make several slits in the top.

Bake for 30 to 35 minutes or until top crust is browned and filling is bubbly. Cool slightly before serving.

Paprika Chicken

Makes 4 servings

2 tablespoons butter

4 chicken breast halves, skinless and boneless

1 10.5-ounce can cream of mushroom soup

1/2 cup milk

1 teaspoon paprika

1/8 teaspoon ground red pepper

1/3 cup sour cream

*1 16-ounce package egg noodles,
   cooked according to package directions*

1/2 teaspoon dried parsley

In a large skillet, melt the butter over medium-high heat. Add the chicken pieces; cook for 10 minutes or until browned on both sides, turning once. Remove chicken and set aside.

In the skillet, combine soup, milk, paprika, and pepper. Heat to boiling. Return chicken to skillet. Lower heat, cover, and simmer for about 30 to 45 minutes or until chicken is tender, stirring often. Stir in sour cream. Heat through.

Serve over noodles. Sprinkle with parsley.

Chicken Cordon Bleu Casserole

Makes 4 to 5 servings

1 16-ounce package penne pasta, cooked and drained

1 cup cooked and chopped chicken breast

1 cup cooked and chopped ham

1/2 cups milk

1 8-ounce package cream cheese, softened at room temperature

2 tablespoons sliced green onions

2 cups shredded Swiss cheese

1 teaspoon salt

1/2 teaspoon fresh ground pepper

1 cup panko bread crumbs

1/2 cup butter, melted

Preheat broiler. Spray a 9″ x 13″ baking dish with cooking spray.

Cook the pasta according to the package directions. Drain and return to the pot. Add chicken and ham, tossing to combine.

In a medium saucepan, combine the milk, cream cheese, and onion over low-medium heat. Cook, stirring frequently, until cheese is melted and mixture is smooth, about 5 minutes. Stir into the pasta mixture. Stir in the Swiss cheese and season with salt and pepper to taste.

Transfer the combined mixture to prepared baking dish. Top evenly with bread crumbs. Pour melted butter over crumbs and broil until browned, about 4 minutes.

Chicken Divan

Makes 6 to 8 servings

12 fresh broccoli stalks, cleaned and ends trimmed
4 tablespoons olive oil, divided use
6 chicken breast halves, skinless and boneless
1 teaspoon salt
1/2 teaspoon freshly ground pepper
1/2 teaspoon garlic powder
1 cup seasoned bread crumbs
2 tablespoons butter, melted
2 10.5-ounce cans cream of chicken soup
1/2 cup mayonnaise
1 teaspoon curry powder
1 teaspoon lemon juice
1 cup shredded sharp Cheddar cheese
2 cups cooked rice

Preheat oven to 350 degrees.

Arrange broccoli in the bottom of a lightly greased 9" x 13" baking pan. Drizzle or mist 2 tablespoons of the olive oil over the broccoli. Bake the broccoli for about 10 to 15 minutes or until tender; set aside.

Brush chicken breast halves evenly with the other 2 tablespoons of olive oil. Sprinkle each chicken piece with the garlic powder, salt, and pepper to season. Place the chicken in the dish and bake for about 20 minutes, turning after 10 minutes. Remove the chicken and place the broccoli in the bottom of the pan. Lay chicken breast halves on top of the broccoli.

Combine the bread crumbs and butter; set aside.

In a small bowl, combine the soup, mayonnaise, curry powder, and lemon juice; spread evenly over the chicken. Top with the cheese and sprinkle with the bread crumbs.

Bake for 25 to 30 minutes.

Serve over rice.

Sour Cream Chicken Enchiladas

Makes 6 servings

- 6 chicken breast halves, boneless and skinless
- 4 tablespoons butter
- 1 teaspoon salt
- 1/2 teaspoon fresh ground pepper
- 1/2 teaspoon seasoning salt
- 1 tablespoon Gebhardt chili powder
- 1/2 teaspoon chipotle chili powder
- 1 teaspoon cumin
- 1 cup grated Monterey Jack cheese
- 2 10-ounce cans Rotel diced tomatoes and green chilies, divided use
- 1 10.5-ounce can cream of chicken soup
- 1 cup sour cream
- 2 tablespoons vegetable oil
- 1 12-count package corn tortillas

Preheat oven to 350 degrees.

In a 9" x 13" baking dish, melt the butter. Place trimmed chicken breasts in a single layer in the dish; season on both sides with the salt, seasoning salt, and pepper. Bake, turning once, for about 20 minutes or until done.

Remove chicken from dish. Cut into bite-size pieces. Place chopped chicken in a medium bowl. Add the chili and chipotle powders, cumin, cheese, and 1 can of the tomatoes and green chilies, mixing well.

In another medium bowl, mix together the soup, the remaining can of tomatoes and green chilies, and the sour cream. Set aside and reserve.

Wipe baking dish clean and coat with cooking spray; set aside.

Pour the oil in a small frying pan over high heat. Set up an assembly line; fry one tortilla turning once until soft, about 15 seconds. Place softened tortilla on plate and spoon a tablespoon of chicken mixture in the middle; roll tightly and place seam side down in prepared dish. Repeat, filling all tortillas, placing seam side down with sides touching.

Pour sour cream sauce mixture over the top of the enchiladas. Top with shredded cheese.

Bake for about 15 to 20 minutes or until bubbling.

King Ranch Casserole

Makes about 8 servings

4 chicken breast halves, skinless and boneless

1 15-ounce can chicken broth

1 tablespoon chicken bouillon or broth concentrate

1 cup water

1 teaspoon salt

1/2 cup finely chopped yellow onion

1/2 cup finely chopped red bell pepper

1 10.5-ounce can cream of chicken soup

1 10.5-ounce can cream of mushroom soup

1 10-ounce can Rotel diced tomatoes and green chilies

2 16-ounce cans chili beans, drained

1 12-count package flour tortillas, cut into 4" pieces

2 cups shredded Colby Jack cheese

Preheat oven to 350 degrees. Coat a 9" x 13" baking dish with cooking spray.

In a large saucepan, combine the broth, bouillon, water, and salt and bring to a boil. Add the chicken and cook for 15 to 20 minutes or until the chicken is cooked through. Using a slotted spoon, remove chicken from cooking liquid and reserve 1 cup of the cooking liquid. Cut chicken into bite-size pieces.

In a clean large saucepan, combine the reserved cooking liquid, onion, bell pepper, soups, diced tomatoes and green chilies, and beans. Mix together and heat through, stirring often.

In prepared baking dish, arrange the following layers: pieces of four tortillas, half the chicken, 1/3 of the soup mixture. Repeat layers, ending with the soup mixture, spreading evenly and to the edges. Cover with the cheese.

Bake for about 20 to 25 minutes or until heated through and bubbly and cheese is melted.

Texas Spicy Chicken Breasts

Makes 4 servings

5 tablespoons butter, divided use

3 medium jalapeño peppers, seeded and sliced

5 cloves garlic, finely chopped

2/3 cup white wine

2 tablespoons lemon juice

2 cups chicken stock

7 tablespoons flour, divided use

1 teaspoon garlic salt

1 teaspoon fresh ground pepper

2 tablespoons olive oil

4 chicken breast halves, boneless and skinless

In a medium saucepan, melt 2 tablespoons butter over medium-high heat. Add jalapeños and garlic; cook until soft. Add the wine and cook until liquid is almost evaporated. Add lemon juice and stock; bring to a simmer.

Meanwhile, in a small saucepan over medium heat, melt 3 tablespoons of the butter. Stir in 3 tablespoons flour and cook, stirring until smooth, about 2 minutes. Add flour mixture to liquid, whisking until smooth and thickened. Simmer for 5 minutes.

In a small shallow dish, mix together the other 4 tablespoons of flour, garlic salt, and pepper. Lightly coat chicken on all sides with the olive oil; reserve remaining oil. Lightly press chicken pieces into flour mixture to coat both sides.

In a large skillet over medium-high heat, heat the remaining oil. Cook chicken until golden brown, about 10 minutes on each side, adding a bit more oil if needed. Cover chicken with sauce.

Slow Cooker Sweet and Sour Chicken
Makes 6 servings

*6 chicken breast halves, skinless and boneless,
    cut into bite-size pieces*

1/2 teaspoon salt

1/2 teaspoon fresh ground pepper

2 tablespoons butter

2 large cloves garlic, finely chopped

1/2 cup sliced and chopped green onions

1/2 cup sugar

1/2 cup ketchup

1/2 cup orange juice

2 tablespoons cornstarch

1/4 cup cider vinegar

1/4 cup soy sauce

1 tablespoon grated fresh ginger

1 20-ounce can pineapple chunks with juice

1 large green bell pepper, seeded and cut into 3/4" pieces

1 large red bell pepper, seeded and cut into 3/4" pieces

3 cups cooked white rice

Season the chicken pieces with the salt and pepper; reserve.

In a medium saucepan, melt the butter over medium heat. Add the garlic, green onions, and chicken to the pan. Brown the chicken, approximately 15 to 20 minutes, turning once.

Combine remaining ingredients except the rice in a slow cooker or crock-pot. Cover and cook on low for 6 hours or high for 4 hours.

Serve over rice.

No-Grill Teriyaki Chicken

Makes 4 servings

4 chicken breast halves, skinless and boneless

1/3 cup soy sauce

1/4 cup cider vinegar

1/4 cup ketchup

1/4 cup packed brown sugar

*1 8-ounce can sliced pineapple,
   drained and juice reserved*

Preheat oven to 375 degrees. Lightly coat a 9″ x 13″ baking dish with cooking spray.

Place chicken breast halves in prepared dish without overlapping.

In a separate dish, combine the soy sauce, vinegar, ketchup, brown sugar, and saved pineapple juice; stir until sugar dissolves. Pour over the chicken.

Bake for 25 to 30 minutes, turning twice so the meat develops a brown glaze on both sides.

Ten minutes before cooking time is up, place one slice of pineapple on top of each chicken breast; bake for 10 minutes longer.

Stir-Fry Cashew Chicken

Makes 4 servings

4 teaspoons cornstarch, divided use

2 tablespoons soy sauce, divided use

2 teaspoons dry sherry

1 teaspoon sugar

1/2 teaspoon Tabasco sauce

1 pound chicken tenders, cut into bite-size pieces

1/2 cup unsalted cashews

2 tablespoons olive oil

2 cups red bell pepper, seeded and thickly sliced

2 cloves garlic, minced

1/2 teaspoon peeled and minced fresh ginger

3 tablespoons thinly sliced green onions

In a small bowl, combine 1 teaspoon cornstarch, 1 tablespoon soy sauce, sherry, sugar, and Tabasco sauce; stir with a whisk until smooth.

In a medium bowl, combine remaining 3 teaspoons of cornstarch and remaining soy sauce. Add the chicken and toss well to coat.

Heat a large non-stick skillet over medium-high heat. Add cashews to pan and cook 3 minutes or until lightly toasted, stirring frequently. Remove from pan. Add oil to pan, swirling to coat. Add chicken mixture to pan; cook for 2 minutes or until lightly browned. Remove chicken and add peppers; cook for 2 minutes. Add garlic and ginger and cook 30 seconds. Add chicken and cornstarch mixture and cook 1 minute or until sauce starts to thicken. Reduce heat and simmer for 8 to 10 minutes until chicken is tender. Sprinkle with cashews and green onions.

Tequila-Glazed Grilled Chicken Breast

Makes 6 servings

1 teaspoon ground cumin

1 teaspoon Gebhardt chili powder

1 teaspoon salt

1/2 teaspoon chipotle chili powder

6 chicken breast halves, boneless and skinless

3/4 cup pineapple juice

1/3 cup tequila

1/4 cup honey

2 teaspoons cornstarch

2 teaspoons water

2 teaspoons grated lime rind

3 tablespoons fresh lime juice

1/4 teaspoon crushed red pepper

Oil as needed for grill

Preheat grill to medium-high heat. If using gas grill, preheat both sides. After preheating, turn off left side.

In a small bowl, combine dry spices. Coat chicken pieces evenly on all sides with spices.

In a small saucepan, combine the pineapple juice, tequila, and honey over medium-high heat. Bring to a boil and cook until liquid is reduced to 3/4 cup of liquid, about 10 minutes.

Combine cornstarch and water in a 1-cup measuring cup, stirring until smooth. Add cornstarch mixture to juice mixture, stirring constantly with a whisk. Bring to a boil and cook for 1 minute. Remove from heat and stir in lime rind and juice and red pepper.

Coat right burner side of grill with cooking spray or brush with oil. Place chicken on grill and cover; grill for 5 minutes on each side, basting with sauce. Move chicken to other side, away from direct flame, cook another 5 minutes on each side, basting occasionally. Chicken is done when juices run clear when pierced with a fork.

Lemon Chicken Picatta
Makes 6 servings

6 chicken breast halves, skinless and boneless, sliced thin

1 teaspoon salt

1/2 teaspoon fresh ground pepper

4 tablespoons flour

2 tablespoons butter, divided use

2 tablespoons olive oil

4 cloves garlic, finely chopped

1 cup dry white wine

1 cup chicken broth

1/3 cup lemon juice

1/4 cup capers, rinsed and drained

2 tablespoons sliced and chopped green onions

1 tablespoon chopped fresh parsley

1 pound linguine, cooked and drained

Cut chicken breast halves into thin slices; reserve.

Stir together flour, salt, and pepper on a plate or in a shallow dish. Place chicken pieces in flour to coat all sides.

In a large skillet, melt the butter and olive oil over medium-high heat. Add garlic and cook for 1 minute; stir in chicken and cook for 10 minutes or until the chicken is lightly browned on both sides. Remove chicken and keep warm.

Add wine to pan and bring to a boil, scraping pan to loosen browned bits. Cook 1 minute or until liquid almost evaporates. Stir in broth and bring to a boil. Cook about 4 minutes; stir in lemon juice, capers, and green onions. Pour over chicken and sprinkle with parsley.

Serve with cooked linguine.

Chicken Picatta with Marsala Sauce

Makes 6 servings

6 chicken breasts, skinless and boneless, sliced thin

4 tablespoons butter, divided use

1 tablespoon chopped dried thyme

1/4 cup finely chopped shallots

4 cloves garlic, finely chopped

2 cups sliced mushrooms

1 teaspoon salt

1/2 teaspoon fresh ground pepper

2 cups flour

2 tablespoons olive oil

2 cups sweet Marsala wine

1/2 cup heavy cream

Cut chicken breasts into thin slices.

In a medium skillet over low heat, melt 2 tablespoons of the butter; add the thyme, shallots, and garlic; heat through. Add mushrooms and season with salt and pepper. Cook until mushrooms are brown; reserve.

Place flour on plate or in shallow dish. Coat chicken slices in flour, shaking off excess.

In a separate large skillet over medium heat, heat olive oil and remaining 2 tablespoons of butter. Add chicken and cook for 10 minutes, until brown on all sides.

Add Marsala to the pan and cook until liquid starts to reduce, about 5 minutes. Add the mushrooms and the cream. Cook until the cream reduces and the sauce is thickened and heated through, about 5 minutes.

Maple-Mustard Glazed Chicken

Makes 4 servings

2 tablespoons olive oil

2 tablespoons butter

4 chicken breasts, skinless and boneless

1 teaspoon salt

1/2 teaspoon fresh ground pepper

1/2 cup chicken broth

1/2 cup maple syrup

2 teaspoon chopped dried thyme

3 cloves garlic, minced

2 tablespoons cider vinegar

2 tablespoons stone-ground mustard

Preheat oven to 400 degrees.

Heat a large ovenproof skillet over medium-high heat. Add oil and butter and swirl to coat. Sprinkle chicken on all sides with salt and pepper. Add chicken to pan and sauté 10 minutes on each side or until browned. Remove chicken from pan; reserve.

Add broth, syrup, thyme, and garlic to pan. Bring to a boil, scraping pan to loosen browned bits. Cook 2 minutes, stirring frequently. Add vinegar and mustard and cook for 1 minute. Return chicken to pan, spooning mixture over chicken. Place in the oven and bake for 10 minutes or until chicken is done.

Simple Roast Chicken

Makes 6 servings

1 medium yellow onion, sliced

2 cloves garlic, cut in half

1/2 cup chicken broth

1 4-pound chicken, giblets and neck removed

2 tablespoons olive oil, divided use

1 teaspoon kosher salt

1/2 teaspoon fresh ground pepper

1 teaspoon seasoning salt

1 pound new potatoes, cut in half

Preheat oven to 450 degrees.

Place the onion, garlic, and broth in the bottom of a roasting pan.

Rinse the chicken and pat dry with paper towels. Tuck the wings under the chicken, and place chicken on top of the onions and garlic. Rub the chicken with 1 tablespoon of the olive oil, and sprinkle with some of the salt, pepper, and seasoning salt.

Arrange the potatoes around the chicken, drizzle with the remaining oil, and sprinkle with the rest of the salt, pepper, and seasoning salt.

Place in oven, turning the potatoes once, for about 50 to 60 minutes or until chicken tests done. Juices should run clear in thick part of thigh or leg when pierced with a fork. Let the chicken rest at least 15 minutes before carving.

Serve with the potatoes and onions.

Citrus-Marinated Roast Chicken

Makes 6 servings

1/4 cup olive oil

6 chicken breasts, boneless and skinless

4 large lemons, divided use

2 large oranges, divided use

8 cloves garlic, finely chopped

3 teaspoons chopped fresh oregano

3 tablespoons soy sauce

1 tablespoons honey

1/2 teaspoon crushed red pepper flakes

1 teaspoon salt

1/2 teaspoon fresh ground pepper

Pour the olive oil in a large 9" x 13" roasting pan and place chicken pieces in a single layer.

Cut one of the lemons into six wedges. Finely grate the yellow peel from another lemon to yield 1 teaspoon grated lemon zest. Squeeze juice from the remaining lemons to yield 2/3 cup juice. Combine the zest and juice in a small bowl.

Cut one of the oranges into eight wedges. Finely grate the orange peel from the remaining orange to yield 1 teaspoon grated orange zest. Squeeze the juice from the orange to yield 1/2 cup juice. Add orange zest and juice to bowl with lemon juice.

Scatter the fruit wedges around the roasting pan, not on top of chicken. Stir the garlic, oregano, soy sauce, honey, and pepper flakes into citrus juice mixture. Pour the marinade evenly over the chicken. Cover baking dish tightly with plastic wrap and refrigerate at least 6, up to 12, hours, turning pieces occasionally

Preheat oven to 375 degrees. Bake for 20 to 25 minutes or until golden brown.

All-Time Favorite Chicken Tenders

Makes 4 to 5 servings

4 chicken breasts, skinless and boneless

1 1/2 cups flour

2 teaspoon Old Bay seasoning, divided use

2 teaspoons salt, divided use

2 teaspoons fresh ground pepper, divided use

2 eggs, lightly beaten

1 cup buttermilk

2 cups vegetable oil

Cut chicken into 2" pieces.

In a shallow bowl, combine the flour, 1 teaspoon Old Bay seasoning, and 1 teaspoon each salt and pepper. In another shallow bowl, combine the eggs, buttermilk, remaining Old Bay seasoning, salt, and pepper. Place chicken pieces in flour to coat all sides. Dip flour-coated chicken into the egg and buttermilk mixture. Dip again in flour. Set aside on waxed paper.

In a large skillet, heat the oil over medium-high heat to 375 degrees. Slowly add the chicken, a few pieces at a time. Do not crowd pan. Cook for 10 minutes on each side or until golden.

This is great with cream gravy (see page 107).

Oven-Fried Chicken

Makes 6 servings

1 cup buttermilk

2 eggs, lightly beaten

6 chicken breasts, skinless and boneless

3/4 cup flour

1 teaspoon salt

1/2 teaspoon fresh ground black pepper

1/2 teaspoon ground red pepper

1/8 teaspoon ground white pepper

1/4 teaspoon ground cumin

Preheat oven to 450 degrees. Line a sheet pan or shallow baking dish with parchment paper.

Combine buttermilk, egg, 1/2 teaspoon salt, and black pepper in a large resealable plastic bag. Add chicken; seal and refrigerate for 1 hour, turning occasionally.

In another resealable plastic bag, shake together flour, 1/2 teaspoon salt, red and white peppers, and cumin. Remove chicken from marinade, shaking off excess. Place one piece at a time into bag with flour, shaking to coat. Place on waxed paper. Repeat until all chicken pieces are coated with flour, shaking off excess.

Place chicken on prepared baking pan. Lightly spray chicken with cooking spray. Bake for 35 minutes or until done, turning every 15 minutes.

Crunchy Baked Chicken

Makes 6 servings

2 cups buttermilk

1/4 cup sour cream

1 1-ounce package ranch dressing and seasoning mix, divided use

1 teaspoon salt

1/2 teaspoon fresh ground pepper

6 chicken breasts, bone-in, skin removed

5 slices white sandwich bread, torn into pieces

Preheat oven to 450 degrees.

In a large bowl whisk together buttermilk, sour cream, 2 tablespoons ranch seasoning mix, salt, and pepper until salt dissolves. Add chicken and toss to coat. Cover tightly with plastic wrap and refrigerate for at least 30 minutes or 1 hour.

Meanwhile, in a food processor, combine bread pieces and remaining ranch seasoning, pulsing to mix until finely ground. Spray a flat baking dish with cooking spray. Spread thin layer of bread-crumb mixture evenly on prepared baking dish and bake, stirring occasionally, until light golden, about 5 minutes. Transfer toasted bread crumbs to shallow dish.

Remove chicken from buttermilk mixture, allowing excess to drip off. Dip in toasted bread crumbs to coat all sides of chicken evenly. Transfer bread-crumb-coated chicken to the baking dish.

Reduce oven temperature to 400 degrees. Bake until chicken is golden brown, about 20 to 25 minutes.

River Road Oven Chicken

Makes 6 servings

6 whole chicken breasts, skin on

1 cup dry white wine

1 tablespoon lemon juice

1 tablespoon salt

1/2 tablespoon fresh ground pepper

3 cloves garlic, finely chopped

1/2 tablespoon paprika

1/4 cup butter, melted

1/4 cup finely chopped sweet yellow onion

1/4 cup finely chopped fresh parsley

Preheat oven at 325 degrees. Coat 9″ x 13″ baking dish with cooking spray.

Place chicken breasts skin side down in prepared baking dish.

In small bowl, blend remaining ingredients and pour over the chicken breasts.

Cover with foil and bake for 1 hour. Remove the foil and turn the chicken breasts skin side up. Increase temperature to 375 degrees and bake 30 minutes, basting 2 or 3 times. Increase temperature to 425 degrees and bake for 30 minutes more.

Chicken and Rice Casserole

Makes 4 servings

1 cup long grain rice, cooked

4 tablespoons butter, melted

1 10.5-ounce can cream of chicken soup

1 10.5-ounce can cream of celery soup

1 10.5-ounce can cream of mushroom soup

1 1/2 cups water

2 cups cooked chicken breast, cubed

Preheat oven to 325 degrees.

In a large bowl, combine butter, soups, and water, stirring until smooth. Spread cooked rice evenly in bottom of 9″ x 13″ ungreased casserole baking dish. Pour half of soup mixture into casserole. Place the cooked chicken in dish and cover with remaining soup mixture.

Bake, uncovered, for 50 to 60 minutes.

Chicken and Broccoli Alfredo

Makes 4 servings

1 8-ounce package linguine

1 cup fresh broccoli florets

2 tablespoons butter

3 cloves garlic, minced

4 chicken breasts, skinless and boneless, cut into bite-size pieces

1 10.5-ounce can cream of mushroom soup

1/2 cup milk

1/4 cup grated Parmesan cheese

1/4 teaspoon fresh ground pepper

Cook linguine according to package directions. Add broccoli for the last 4 minutes of cooking time and drain.

In a large skillet, melt the butter over medium-high heat. Add chicken and garlic and cook until browned, about 10 minutes. Add soup, milk, cheese, and pepper; stir to evenly coat ingredients. Add the linguine, stir again, and heat through.

CHICKEN ALFREDO WITH CRISPY BACON

Makes 6 servings

1 16-ounce package fettuccine, cooked according to package directions and drained

10 slices bacon

6 chicken breasts, boneless and skinless, cut into bite-size pieces

1 teaspoon salt

1/2 teaspoon fresh ground pepper

8 tablespoons butter, divided use

2 tablespoons chicken broth

4 cloves garlic, finely chopped

2 cups heavy cream

1/4 cup shredded Parmesan cheese

In a large skillet over medium-high heat, cook the bacon until crisp; crumble and set aside, reserving the drippings.

Season chicken pieces with salt and pepper. Melt 1 tablespoon butter in the skillet with the drippings over medium heat. Add chicken broth and chicken; cook until lightly browned, about 15 minutes.

Stir in garlic and cook another 5 minutes. Add the remaining 7 tablespoons butter and cream. Bring to a boil and simmer until butter melts and mixture begins to thicken, about 5 minutes, stirring frequently. Stir in cheese and cook until melted and mixture thickens, about 3 to 5 minutes. Add fettuccine, mixing to coat pasta. Top with bacon.

Chicken Florentine Pasta

Makes 6 servings

4 tablespoons olive oil, divided use
6 chicken breasts, skinless and boneless
1 teaspoon salt
1/2 teaspoon fresh ground pepper
1 16-ounce package linguine
3 tablespoons flour
4 cloves garlic, minced
1 cup milk
1 cup chicken broth
1/2 cup grated Parmesan cheese
4 cups fresh spinach leaves, torn into pieces

In a large skillet, heat 2 tablespoons of the oil over medium-high heat.

Season the chicken on all sides with the salt and pepper. Place chicken in pan and cook for about 8 minutes on each side or until done. Remove chicken; carve into thin slices.

Cook the pasta according to the package directions. Drain and keep warm.

In a large non-stick skillet, heat remaining 2 tablespoons of olive oil over medium heat, swirling pan to coat bottom evenly. Add flour and garlic; cook until garlic is browned, about 2 minutes, stirring constantly. Using a whisk, stir in the milk and broth. Lower heat and simmer liquid for about 2 minutes or until thickened. Add cheese, stirring until cheese melts. Add the spinach and stir until spinach wilts. Add pasta and chicken, stirring to coat pasta evenly.

In this recipe, chicken breasts may be grilled instead of sautéed.

Easy Chicken with Thin Spaghetti

Makes 6 to 8 servings

1/2 cup butter
4 cups sliced fresh mushrooms
1/2 cup flour
2 cups chicken broth
1 cup milk
2 cups cooked chicken breast, cut in bite-size pieces
1 teaspoon salt
1/2 teaspoon fresh ground pepper
1/2 cup grated Parmesan cheese
16 ounces thin spaghetti, cooked according to package directions, drained
1 tablespoon finely chopped dried parsley

In a 3-quart saucepan, melt butter over medium-high heat. Add mushrooms and sauté until wilted. Blend in flour to evenly coat mushrooms. Gradually stir in chicken broth and milk. Cook over low heat, stirring often, until sauce thickens.

Add chicken, salt, and pepper. Stir in cheese. Heat through but do not allow to boil. Serve sauce over hot cooked spaghetti. Sprinkle with the parsley.

Swiss Cheese Chicken

Makes 6 servings

6 chicken breast halves, boneless and skinless
8 slices packaged Swiss cheese, unwrapped
1 10.5-ounce can cream of chicken soup
1/4 cup white wine
1 cup herb-seasoned stuffing mix
1/4 cup butter, melted

Preheat oven to 350 degrees. Coat a 9" x 13" glass baking with cooking spray.

Pound chicken pieces until 1/4" thick. Arrange chicken in single layer in prepared baking dish. Place cheese over top of each breast, covering holes.

In a small bowl, combine soup and wine; spoon over chicken. Sprinkle stuffing evenly over soup mixture. Pour melted butter over top of stuffing.

Bake for 50 to 55 minutes.

Serve with wild rice.

Roast Turkey

Makes 12 to 20 servings

1 15- to 20-pound whole turkey
1 turkey-size oven roasting bag
1/2 cup butter, cut into tablespoon-size pieces
1 onion, cut into four pieces
1 pint chicken broth
Salt and pepper to taste

Coat a large turkey roasting pan with cooking spray. Rinse the turkey; remove bag with giblets and neck; discard.

Place the turkey in the oven bag. Place tablespoons of butter around and inside the turkey. Tear apart the onion and place pieces around and inside the turkey. Pour chicken broth inside and around turkey. Sprinkle with salt and pepper to taste. Close bag and cook according to oven bag instructions.

Remove turkey from bag and keep warm while preparing gravy.

Strain pan juices into a large saucepan and reserve for gravy. (see page 108)

Impress everyone with this Thanksgiving turkey dinner.

Turkey Tenderloins with Sweet Chili Sauce

Makes 6 servings

2 tablespoons sugar
2 teaspoon salt
1 teaspoon fresh ground pepper
2 teaspoons ground cinnamon
2 teaspoons garlic powder
1 teaspoon dried thyme leaves, crushed
1/2 teaspoon ground cumin

1 24-ounce package boneless turkey breast tenderloins
2 tablespoons olive oil, divided use
2 15-ounce cans chicken broth
1/2 cup Asian-style sweet chili sauce
1 tablespoon Worcestershire sauce

Preheat oven to 350 degrees, if finishing dish in oven. Or have a slow cooker ready.

In small bowl, stir together sugar, salt, pepper, cinnamon, garlic powder, thyme, and cumin. Brush turkey with 1 tablespoon of the olive oil. Rub turkey with sugar mixture, coating all sides evenly.

In a medium skillet, heat remaining oil over medium-high heat. Add turkey and cook for 15 minutes or until brown on all sides. Place turkey and the broth in a 9″ square baking dish, cover, and bake for about 15 to 20 minutes.

If using a slow cooker, place seasoned turkey and broth in slow cooker on low for 5 to 6 hours or until it is done and very tender.

Stir together chili sauce and Worcestershire sauce; heat through before serving.

When turkey is done, slice and serve with sauce.

This tangy dish may be baked in the oven or simmered in a slow cooker.

Main Dishes

~ Seafood ~

TIP

Always buy fresh fish the day you
prepare it to insure freshness.

Grilled Lobster Tails

Makes 4 servings

4 lobster tails in the shell
2 tablespoons butter, melted
Juice of 1/2 lemon
Lemon slices
Additional melted butter for dipping cooked lobster

Preheat grill to medium.

Cut down the center of the underside of the lobster tails with a pair of kitchen shears to expose the meat. Peel away the tail cartilage from the underside to leave the meat exposed.

Combine melted butter and lemon juice; brush on the exposed tail meat. Place lobster tails, meat side down, on grill. Cook for approximately 10 minutes, watching closely. Flip tails and cook 3 to 5 minutes on the shell side. Tails will curl when they are done. Remove from grill. Serve with sliced lemon and melted butter for dipping.

Beer Batter Fried Seafood

Makes enough batter for 6 to 8 servings

1 12-ounce can of beer
1 1/2 cups cornmeal
1 teaspoon salt
1/2 teaspoon fresh ground pepper
1 teaspoon Old Bay seasoning
1/2 teaspoon paprika
Vegetable oil
Shrimp or white fish cut into serving-size pieces

In a medium bowl, combine beer and dry ingredients, mixing until smooth.

In a skillet, heat 2 inches of cooking oil to 375 degrees over medium-high heat. Dip shrimp or fish pieces into the batter. Shake off excess. Carefully lower battered fish or shrimp into hot oil and cook in small batches until golden, about 3 to 5 minutes.

Grilled Shrimp Brochettes

Makes 6 servings

1/2 cup olive oil

2 tablespoons Cajun seasoning

1 tablespoon fresh lemon juice

24 colossal-size shrimp, peeled and deveined

6 jalapeño peppers, seeded and cut into 2" strips

8 ounces Monterey Jack cheese, cut into 1/2" cubes

24 thin slices bacon

24 wooden skewers, soaked in water for 30 minutes

In a large resealable plastic bag, combine the olive oil, Cajun seasoning, and lemon juice. Add shrimp and toss well so that all shrimp are covered with marinade. Seal and refrigerate 9 hours or overnight.

Preheat grill to medium.

Line curve of each shrimp with a strip of the jalapeño and a couple of cheese cubes. Wrap each shrimp with a slice of bacon. Thread onto skewer to secure bacon around ingredients.

Grill for about 8 to 10 minutes, turning several times, until bacon is crisp at the edges.

New Orleans-Style Barbecued Shrimp

Makes 4 servings

1 tablespoon canola oil

3 tablespoons sliced and finely chopped green onions

2 tablespoons dry white wine

3 cloves garlic, finely chopped

4 tablespoons Worcestershire sauce

1 teaspoon Tabasco sauce

1 teaspoon salt

1/2 teaspoon fresh ground black pepper

1/2 teaspoon ground red pepper

1/2 teaspoon paprika

1 cup salted butter, cut into small pieces

20 large shrimp, peeled and deveined

Slices of warm French bread

In a large heavy saucepan, heat the oil over high heat. Cook shrimp until they just barely turn pink. Remove shrimp and set aside on a large platter. Add green onions and cook for 1 minute. Add the white wine and cook until it is reduced by half.

Add the garlic, Worcestershire sauce, Tabasco sauce, salt, black pepper, red pepper, and paprika. Cook for 1 minute stirring constantly. Reduce the heat to low. Slowly add butter pieces to the pan, stirring constantly.

Return shrimp to the pan and toss well to coat shrimp with the butter and seasonings and to heat through.

Serve with warm French bread to soak up the spicy butter.

Garlicky Grilled Shrimp

Makes 4 servings

2 tablespoons olive oil
2 tablespoons butter, melted
1/2 cup sliced and finely chopped green onions
8 cloves garlic, minced
1/4 tablespoons dry white wine
2 tablespoons fresh lime juice
2 tablespoons chopped dried parsley
24 extra-large shrimp, shelled and deveined, tails off
1 teaspoon salt
1/2 teaspoon fresh ground pepper
3 tablespoons unsalted butter, softened

In a large bowl, mix together the oil, butter, onions, garlic, wine, lime juice, and parsley. Season the shrimp with the salt and pepper and add to the bowl. Let stand for 15 to 20 minutes.

Thread the shrimp onto four skewers and rub the butter all over the shrimp. Brush the grate with a little olive oil. Grill the shrimp over medium-high heat, basting with the marinade and turning until just cooked through, about 7 to 8 minutes.

Grilled Bourbon-Basted Salmon

Makes 4 servings

4 6-ounce salmon fillets, skin removed
1/4 cup packed brown sugar
1/4 cup Wild Turkey bourbon whiskey
1/4 cup soy sauce
1/4 cup vegetable oil
1/4 cup sliced and finely chopped green onions

Arrange the salmon in a single layer in a shallow glass dish. Combine the brown sugar, bourbon, soy sauce, oil, and green onions in a bowl and mix well. Pour over the salmon, turning to coat. Marinate, covered, in refrigerator for 1 hour, turning occasionally.

Meanwhile preheat a gas grill to medium high.

Drain the salmon, reserving the marinade. Place the salmon in a grilling basket. Grill over hot coals for 7 minutes per side or until the salmon flakes easily, turning and basting with the reserved marinade several times.

Apple and Horseradish-Glazed Salmon

Makes 4 servings

1/3 cup apple jelly

1 tablespoon finely chopped green onions

2 tablespoons prepared horseradish

1 tablespoon white wine vinegar

1 teaspoon salt

1/2 teaspoon fresh ground pepper

2 tablespoons olive oil

2 tablespoons butter

4 6-ounce salmon fillets, cut 1" thick

Preheat oven to 350 degrees.

In a small bowl, combine the jelly, green onions, horseradish, vinegar, salt, and pepper; reserve.

In a large ovenproof skillet, heat the oil and butter over medium-high heat. Sprinkle fillets on both sides with salt and pepper. Place fillets in pan and cook 5 minutes. Turn fillets over and brush with half of the apple jelly mixture.

Place skillet in oven for 5 minutes or until fish flakes easily. Brush with remaining apple jelly mixture.

Salmon with Garlic Butter

Makes 4 servings

1 cup dry white wine

2 teaspoons lemon juice

6 tablespoons butter, cut into pieces

1 teaspoon salt

1/2 teaspoon fresh ground pepper

2 cloves garlic, crushed

4 6-ounce salmon fillets, skin-on

2 tablespoons olive oil

2 tablespoons butter

In a small saucepan, simmer the wine with the lemon juice over medium-high heat until reduced to 1 tablespoon, about 8 to 10 minutes. Reduce the heat to low and whisk in the butter, one tablespoon at a time, until sauce starts to thicken. Whisk in the garlic, salt, and pepper. Keep sauce warm.

In a large skillet or sauté pan, heat the olive oil and butter over medium-high heat. Season the salmon fillets with salt and pepper. Cook skin side down over medium-high heat, turning once until browned and cooked through, about 10 to 12 minutes. Cook in batches, if necessary. Do not crowd pan. Keep warm until all fillets are cooked.

Spoon garlic butter sauce over the salmon and serve.

Pan-Roasted Salmon

Makes 4 servings

- 1/2 cup whiskey
- 1/4 cup pineapple juice
- 2 tablespoons cider vinegar
- 1 tablespoon finely chopped shallots
- 2 teaspoons paprika
- 1 teaspoon finely chopped garlic
- 1 teaspoon chipotle chili powder
- 1 tablespoon honey
- 1 tablespoon tomato paste
- 1 tablespoon Worcestershire sauce
- 8 tablespoons unsalted butter, cold and cut into pieces
- 2 tablespoons brown sugar
- 2 teaspoons kosher salt
- 1 teaspoon fresh ground pepper
- 1/2 teaspoon ground cumin
- 1/4 teaspoon dry mustard
- 1/8 teaspoon ground cinnamon
- 4 4-ounce salmon fillets, skin-on
- 1 tablespoon olive oil

Preheat oven to 350 degrees.

In a small saucepan, combine whiskey, pineapple juice, vinegar, shallots, paprika, garlic, and chipotle chili powder over medium-high heat. Bring to a boil and cook until liquid is reduced. Stir in honey, tomato paste, and Worcestershire sauce. Turn off the heat, whisk in butter a few cubes at a time until butter is melted and well-blended. Season with salt and pepper. Reserve and keep warm.

For the salmon, combine brown sugar, salt, pepper, cumin, mustard, and cinnamon in a small bowl; rub on the top side of the salmon fillets. In a large oven-safe skillet or sauté pan, heat olive oil over high heat. Add fillets to skillet and cook until brown, about 2 minutes. Turn the fillets skin side down and transfer the skillet to the oven. Roast until fillets flake easily with a fork, 5 to 6 minutes.

Serve with warm sauce.

GRILLED SALMON

Makes 6 servings

6 4- to 6-ounce salmon fillets, skinless
3 tablespoons olive oil
1 tablespoon lemon juice
1 clove garlic, finely chopped
1 teaspoon salt
1/2 teaspoon fresh ground pepper
1 teaspoon finely chopped fresh parsley
Additional vegetable oil as needed for grill

Arrange salmon fillets in a single layer in a shallow glass dish.

In a small bowl, whisk together the olive oil, lemon juice, garlic, salt, pepper, and parsley. Pour over the salmon to coat all sides. Place in the refrigerator for 10 to 15 minutes.

Preheat gas grill to high. Brush grill rack with oil; reduce the heat to medium. Arrange the salmon diagonally on the rack and close the lid. Grill for 5 minutes. Turn the fillets to face the opposite direction to ensure nice grill marks. Grill for 5 minutes longer or until the fish is flaky.

Salmon Patties

Makes 6 to 8 patties

2 6-ounce cans/packages pink salmon, skinless and boneless, drained
3 tablespoons finely chopped yellow onion
2 tablespoons Worcestershire sauce
1 teaspoon salt
1/2 teaspoon fresh ground pepper
1 egg, beaten
1/3 cup milk
15 saltine crackers, crushed
4 tablespoons vegetable oil

In a medium bowl, empty salmon, breaking it apart with a fork. Add the onion, Worcestershire sauce, salt, and pepper. In a small bowl, beat egg with milk and add to salmon. Mix well with clean hands. Add the crushed crackers and make into fist-size flattened patties.

In a large skillet, heat oil over medium-high heat. Place patties in the hot oil and cook until brown on both sides, about 5 to 6 minutes on each side, approximately 10 to 15 minutes.

This simple recipe is my daughter's favorite.

OVEN-FRIED HALIBUT

Makes 4 servings

2 tablespoons vegetable oil

1 cup flour

1 teaspoon fresh ground pepper

1 cup lager-style beer

2 tablespoons creamy mustard blend such as Dijonnaise

2 tablespoons fresh lime juice

2 large eggs, lightly beaten

1 cup panko bread crumbs

1 teaspoon chipotle chili powder

1 teaspoon Old Bay seasoning

1 teaspoon salt

4 6-ounce halibut fillets

Preheat oven to 425 degrees. Coat a rimmed baking sheet with cooking spray and spread evenly with oil. Place baking sheet in oven for 10 minutes.

Combine flour with pepper in a shallow dish.

Combine beer, mustard, lime juice, and eggs in another shallow dish. Stir with whisk until foamy.

Place panko bread crumbs, chipotle chili powder, and Old Bay seasoning in a food processor and pulse for a few seconds until coarse crumbs form. Place in another shallow dish.

Sprinkle fish evenly on all sides with the salt. Dip each piece of fish in flour mixture, then in egg mixture, and then into bread crumb mixture until completely covered. Place fish on preheated baking sheet and bake for 15 to 20 minutes, turning once.

Pan-Seared Halibut with Bell Pepper Relish

Makes 4 servings

4 tablespoons olive oil, divided use

2 tablespoons butter

4 6-ounce halibut fillets

1 teaspoon salt

1/2 teaspoon fresh ground pepper

2 tablespoons sliced and finely chopped green onions

2 cloves garlic, finely chopped

1/2 cup chopped yellow bell pepper

1/2 cup chopped green bell pepper

1/2 cup seeded and chopped Roma tomatoes

1 tablespoon sherry vinegar

1/2 teaspoon paprika

1 tablespoon chopped fresh parsley

In a large skillet, heat 2 tablespoons of the olive oil and the butter over medium-high heat.

Season halibut on all sides with the salt and pepper. Add the fish to pan and cook 4 to 5 minutes on each side or until fish flakes easily. Remove fish from pan with a flat spatula; keep warm.

Add remaining 2 tablespoons of the olive oil to the skillet. Add the green onions and garlic; cook for 1 minute. Add the yellow and green bell peppers, tomato, vinegar, and paprika; cook for 3 minutes or until bell pepper is tender. Stir in parsley. Serve with fish.

CORNFLAKE-CRUSTED HALIBUT WITH CHILI-CILANTRO SAUCE

Makes 4 servings

2 tablespoons finely chopped fresh cilantro

3 tablespoons mayonnaise

1 small serrano chili, seeded and finely chopped

1 clove garlic, minced

1 cup milk

1 large egg, lightly beaten

2 cups cornflakes, finely crushed

1/4 cups flour

1 teaspoon salt

1/2 teaspoon fresh ground pepper

2 tablespoons olive oil

2 tablespoons butter

4 6-ounce halibut fillets

2 tablespoons fresh lemon juice

In a small bowl, combine cilantro, mayonnaise, serrano chili, and garlic, mixing well. Refrigerate to blend flavors.

In a shallow bowl, combine the milk and egg, mixing well. In another shallow bowl or pan, combine the cornflakes, flour, salt, and pepper.

In a large non-stick skillet, heat the oil and the butter over medium-high heat. Dip each fillet in the milk mixture and then the cornflake mixture, coating evenly. Place fillets in pan and cook for 4 to 5 minutes on each side or until fish flakes easily. Sprinkle with lemon juice.

Serve with the chili-cilantro sauce.

Pecan-Crusted Tilapia or Trout

Makes 4 servings

1/2 cup panko bread crumbs

2 tablespoons finely chopped pecans

1/2 teaspoon garlic powder

1 teaspoon salt

1 teaspoon finely chopped parsley

1/2 teaspoon fresh ground pepper

3 tablespoons flour

1/2 cup buttermilk

1/2 teaspoon Tabasco sauce

4 6-ounce tilapia or trout fillets, skin-on

1 tablespoon vegetable oil

1 tablespoon butter

1 tablespoon fresh lemon juice

Preheat oven to 350 degrees. Line a rimmed sheet pan with parchment paper.

In a shallow dish, combine bread crumbs, pecans, garlic powder, parsley, salt, and pepper. Place the flour in another shallow dish. In a small bowl, combine the buttermilk and Tabasco.

Dip each fillet in the flour to coat all sides. Then dip into the buttermilk. Press both sides of fillets into the pecan mixture to coat evenly. Repeat for each fillet.

In a small saucepan, melt the butter over low heat; add the olive oil. Place fillets on lined pan. Pour butter and olive oil mixture evenly over the fish.

Place in oven and bake fish for 4 to 5 minutes. Turn fillets and bake additional 4 to 5 minutes or until fish flakes easily and crust is brown.

Squeeze lemon juice over fillets when ready to serve.

BLACKENED TILAPIA

Makes 4 servings

2 teaspoons paprika

2 teaspoons brown sugar

1 teaspoon dried oregano

1 teaspoon garlic powder

1/2 teaspoon salt

1/2 teaspoon ground cumin

1/4 teaspoon ground red pepper

4 6-ounce tilapia fillets, boneless and skinless

2 tablespoons vegetable oil

In a small bowl, combine all ingredients except fish and oil to make seasoning mixture. Season fillets evenly on all sides.

In a large skillet, heat oil over medium-high heat. Add fish to pan and cook 4 to 5 minutes on each side or until fish flakes easily.

Grilled Grouper with Soy-Ginger Glaze

Makes 4 servings

5 tablespoons soy sauce

1 tablespoon grated fresh ginger

1 tablespoon Worcestershire sauce

3 tablespoons honey

1 tablespoon white wine vinegar

3 tablespoons water

2 teaspoons cornstarch mixed with 2 teaspoons water

3 tablespoons cold butter

4 6-ounce fresh grouper fillets, boneless and skinless

1 teaspoon salt

1/2 teaspoon pepper

1/2 cup coconut milk

Preheat gas grill to medium high.

In a small saucepan, combine the soy sauce, ginger, Worcestershire sauce, honey, vinegar, and 3 tablespoons water over medium-low heat, stirring until heated through. Stir in the cornstarch mixture, cooking and stirring until mixture is bubbly and slightly thickened. Remove from heat and cool slightly. Whisk in chilled butter, 1 tablespoon at a time, stirring constantly.

Season fillets evenly on all sides with salt and pepper. Spoon half the butter mixture over the fillets. Brush grill with oil and grill the fillets over medium-high heat for about 5 minutes on each side or until the fish flakes easily.

Mix the remaining warm glaze with the coconut milk and drizzle around the grilled fish.

Main Dishes

~ Pork ~

TIP

Set up your kitchen for easy
flow while cooking.

Barbecued Pulled Pork

Makes 6 to 8 sandwiches

1 tablespoon vegetable oil

4- to 5-pound pork tenderloin, trimmed

1 teaspoon garlic powder

1 teaspoon salt

1 teaspoon fresh ground pepper

1 cup beef broth

1 cup water

Barbecue sauce (see page 98)

Toasted buns, sliced red onions, and deli pickles

In a Dutch oven, heat oil over medium-high heat. Cook pork until brown on all sides. Season meat evenly on all sides with the garlic powder, salt, and pepper.

In a large crock-pot, combine browned pork roast with the broth and water. Cook for 8 to 10 hours on high setting.

When meat is very tender, carefully remove from crock-pot. Cool enough to handle and tear the meat into shreds.

To serve, warm some barbecue sauce in clean Dutch oven. Add pork and stir to coat meat evenly. Add additional sauce as desired and heat through.

Serve on toasted buns with sliced red onions and deli pickles.

This tangy pork is great on sesame seed sandwich buns.

Baja Pork Stir-Fry

Makes 4 servings

1/4 cup chicken broth

1 teaspoon cornstarch

1/2 teaspoon ground cumin

2 cloves garlic, finely chopped

1 2- to 3-pound pork tenderloin, cut into 1" strips

1 teaspoon salt

1/2 teaspoon fresh ground pepper

2 tablespoons olive oil

2 tablespoons butter

1/2 medium red onion, sliced 1/2" thick

1/2 cup yellow bell pepper, sliced 1/2" thick

1/2 cup green bell pepper, sliced 1/2" thick

1/2 cup red bell pepper, sliced 1/2" thick

1 jalapeño pepper, seeded and finely chopped

10 cherry tomatoes, cut in half

2 tablespoons chopped fresh cilantro

In an 8-ounce measuring cup, combine the chicken broth, cornstarch, cumin, and garlic; reserve.

Season pork strips evenly on all sides with the salt and pepper.

In a large skillet, heat the olive oil and butter over medium-high heat. Add pork and sauté 5 minutes or until browned on all sides. Remove and keep warm.

Heat pan over high heat; add onion and cook for 1 minute, stirring frequently. Add the peppers and jalapeño; cook and stir another minute. Stir in reserved broth mixture and bring to a boil. Adjust seasoning with salt and pepper to taste. Remove from heat and stir in tomatoes and sprinkle with cilantro. Pour sauce over the pork strips.

Mushroom Pork Chops

Makes 5 to 6 servings

10 center-cut pork chops, trimmed and sliced thin

2 tablespoons vegetable oil

1 tablespoon butter

1 teaspoon salt

1/2 teaspoon fresh ground pepper

1 teaspoon garlic powder

2 10.5-ounce cans cream of mushroom soup

1 cup milk

3 tablespoons Worcestershire sauce

2 cups cooked rice

In a large skillet with a lid, heat oil and butter over medium-high heat. Season each chop evenly on all sides with the salt, pepper, and garlic powder. Place chops in pan and cook until brown on both sides, approximately 3 to 4 minutes on each side. Remove and set aside.

Add the soup to the skillet with the milk and the Worcestershire sauce, stirring to combine. Place pork chops back in the skillet. Stir well and cover. Turn down heat and simmer for an hour, stirring frequently. Serve over rice.

Another family favorite in the Hensel dinner rotation.

Honey-Garlic Pork Chops

Makes 6 servings

1/4 cup lemon juice

1/4 cup honey

2 tablespoons soy sauce

1 tablespoon dry sherry

2 cloves garlic, finely chopped

6 boneless center-cut pork loin chops, 1" thick

2 tablespoons olive oil

2 tablespoons butter

In a small bowl, combine lemon juice, honey, soy sauce, dry sherry, and garlic. Place the chops in a large resealable plastic bag and pour marinade over chops. Seal and shake to evenly coat chops. Refrigerate for 4 to 6 hours.

Remove chops from marinade; reserve marinade.

In a large skillet, combine olive oil and butter over medium-high heat. Place the chops in the pan, cooking for 10 to 15 minutes on each side. Baste with the reserved marinade. Do not overcook.

Pork Medallions with Lemon-Garlic Sauce

Makes 6 servings

6 pork tenderloin chops, trimmed and cut into 1" cubes

1 teaspoon salt

1 teaspoon fresh ground pepper

2 tablespoons olive oil

2 tablespoons butter

2 cloves garlic, finely chopped

1/2 cup dry white wine

1/2 cup chicken broth

1 tablespoon lemon juice

1 tablespoon chopped fresh parsley

Season pork evenly on all sides with salt and pepper.

In a medium skillet, heat the olive oil and butter over medium-high heat. Add pork and sauté for about 5 to 7 minutes or until brown on all sides. Remove pork and keep warm.

Stir garlic into pan and cook about 30 seconds. Add wine and broth. Increase to high heat, cooking about 5 minutes, stirring to scrape browned bits from bottom of the skillet. Remove skillet from heat and stir in the juice and parsley. Adjust seasoning with salt and pepper.

Serve medallions drizzled with sauce.

Slow-Roasted Pork Tenderloin with Cranberry Sauce
Makes 5 to 6 servings

1 teaspoon dried sage

1 teaspoon dried thyme

1 teaspoon garlic salt

1 teaspoon fresh ground pepper

1 3- to 4-pound pork tenderloin, trimmed

2 tablespoons olive oil

2 tablespoons butter

2 cups chicken broth, divided use

2 14-ounce cans whole berry cranberry sauce

1 cup cranberry juice cocktail

2 tablespoons grape jelly

In a small bowl, combine sage, thyme, garlic salt, and pepper and rub evenly over pork.

In a large Dutch oven, heat the oil and butter over medium-high heat. Add pork and cook on all sides until brown, about 10 minutes. Place pork roast in slow cooker with 1 cup of the chicken broth and cook on low heat for about 4 to 6 hours or until meat is easily pierced with a fork.

Add remaining cup of broth, cranberry sauce, and cranberry juice to Dutch oven. Bring to a boil, scraping pan to loosen browned bits in bottom of the pan. Stir in the jelly and simmer 10 minutes or until mixture is slightly thick, stirring occasionally.

Pour sauce over pork and serve.

Pork Chops with Bourbon-Glazed Onions

Makes 6 servings

4 tablespoons butter, divided use

2 cups sliced yellow onions, 1/4" thick

2 teaspoons sugar

1/3 cup bourbon

1/4 cup toasted pecans, finely chopped

1 tablespoon finely chopped fresh sage

6 6-ounce center-cut pork chops

1 teaspoon garlic salt

1/2 teaspoon fresh ground pepper

2 tablespoons olive oil

In a large skillet with lid, melt 2 tablespoons of the butter over medium-high heat. Add the onions and sugar; cook and stir for 1 minute. Cover pan, reduce heat to medium-low, and simmer onions about 10 more minutes.

Remove lid and stir onions, scraping up brown bits from the pan. Cook onions, uncovered, until they are very brown and caramelized, about 10 more minutes. Add the bourbon and cook until almost evaporated, about 2 to 3 minutes more. Transfer onions to a bowl; stir in the pecans and sage; reserve and keep warm.

Season chops evenly on all sides with garlic salt and pepper. Wipe out skillet and heat the olive oil and the other 2 tablespoons of butter over medium heat. Add chops and cook until brown, about 5 minutes on each side. Cover pan, reduce heat to low, and cook chops about 7 to 10 minutes longer. Add onions and heat through.

Dry-Rubbed Babyback Ribs

Make 5 to 6 servings

3 teaspoons garlic powder

2 tablespoons brown sugar

1 teaspoon Gebhardt chili powder

1/2 teaspoon ground red pepper

2 teaspoons salt

1 teaspoon fresh ground black pepper

2 racks babyback ribs

In a small bowl, combine the garlic powder, sugar, chili powder, red pepper, salt, and black pepper. Rub mixture over the ribs and let sit for 20 to 30 minutes.

Heat gas grill to medium. Place the ribs in a roasting pan and grill in roasting pan, turning occasionally. Bake for 1 1/2 to 2 hours or until done.

Baked Ham

Makes 6 to 8 servings

1 5- to 6-pound whole cooked boneless ham, sliced 1/4" thick

1 20-ounce can crushed pineapple

2 cups brown sugar

Preheat oven to 350 degrees.

Arrange ham slices in a large Dutch oven.

In a small bowl, combine the pineapple and brown sugar, mixing well. Pour over ham, making sure sauce gets in between the slices. Cook for 45 minutes or until ham is heated through.

This is a great dish for a lazy Sunday or an Easter celebration. Boar's Head Brand Sweet Slice ham is our favorite to use in this recipe.

Slow Cooker Cherry-Cola Ham

Makes about 6 to 8 servings

1 cup packed brown sugar

2/3 cup cherry cola

2 tablespoons lemon juice

1 tablespoon dry mustard

1 5- to 6-pound whole cooked boneless ham

1/4 cup cold water

2 tablespoons cornstarch

1 tablespoon prepared horseradish

In a slow cooker, combine brown sugar, cola, lemon juice, and mustard, stirring until sugar is dissolved. Add ham, turning to coat all sides. Cover and cook on low heat for 8 to 10 hours. Remove ham and keep warm.

In a small saucepan, stir together the water and cornstarch until smooth. Add cooking liquid from slow cooker. Cook and stir over medium heat until thickened and bubbly. Cook and stir for 2 minutes more. Blend in horseradish.

Slice ham and serve with sauce.

Desserts

~ Cookies ~

TIP

Especially when baking, use the listed
ingredients in a recipe. Substitutions
can change the result.

Old-Fashioned Butter Cookies

Makes 4 dozen cookies

2 cups sugar

1 cup butter, softened at room temperature

1 teaspoon salt

1 cup buttermilk

1 teaspoon ground nutmeg

1 teaspoon baking soda

1 teaspoon vanilla

2 eggs, beaten

4 1/2 cups flour

1 teaspoon baking powder

Colored sugar for decoration

Preheat oven to 400 degrees. Grease a cookie sheet with shortening or coat with cooking spray.

In a large bowl with a handheld mixer, beat together the butter and sugar on high speed until smooth and creamy.

With beaters on low speed, add remaining ingredients except flour and baking powder. When mixture is smooth, slowly add flour and baking powder, blending with a spoon. Batter should be stiff but smooth.

Drop batter by tablespoons onto greased cookie sheet, about 2 inches apart. Flatten with a fork dipped in water, making a crisscross pattern on top. Sprinkle top surface of cookies with colored sugar. Bake for 8 minutes or until cookies are brown around the edges. Repeat until all dough has been used.

Momo's No-Roll Sugar Cookies

Makes 4 dozen cookies

1 cup margarine, not butter

2 cups sugar

2 eggs

1 1/2 teaspoons vanilla

4 cups flour

1 teaspoon cream of tartar

3/4 teaspoon baking soda

1/2 teaspoon salt

Colored sugar for decoration

Preheat oven to 375 degrees.

In a large bowl with a handheld mixer, beat together the margarine and sugar on high speed until smooth and creamy. With beaters on low speed, add eggs and vanilla, mixing until smooth.

Slowly add flour, cream of tartar, baking soda, and salt, blending on low speed or with a spoon.

Drop batter by rounded teaspoons onto ungreased cookie sheet. Flatten with a fork dipped in water, making a crisscross pattern on top. Sprinkle top surface of cookies with colored sugar. Bake for 7 to 8 minutes or until slightly browned around edges. Repeat until all dough has been used.

Everyone needs great memories of the family in the kitchen making cookies.

Roll-Out Sugar Cookies for Santa

Makes 4 dozen cookies

1 egg, beaten	3/4 cup sugar
1/4 cup vegetable shortening	1 teaspoon vanilla
1/4 cup butter, softened at room temperature	1 1/4 cups flour
	1/4 teaspoon salt
1 tablespoon plus 2 to 4 teaspoons milk (or as needed), divided use	1/4 teaspoon baking powder
	1 cup powdered sugar

In large bowl with a handheld mixer, beat together egg, shortening, butter, and sugar. Mix until smooth. Stir in milk and vanilla.

Blend in flour, salt, and baking powder on low speed or with spoon. Cover and place in refrigerator until dough is firm, approximately 30 minutes.

Preheat oven to 400 degrees. Coat a cookie sheet with cooking spray.

Divide dough into four parts, working with one part at a time. Store remaining dough in refrigerator. The dough will become sticky and hard to work with if it is not cold.

On a pastry mat or board dusted with flour, roll dough with floured rolling pin to 1/8″ thick. Cut out with desired cookie cutters. Use spatula to move cookie cut-outs to prepared cookie sheet, a couple of inches apart. Bake for 3 to 5 minutes or until edges are a touch of brown; watch carefully.

Repeat with remaining dough until all cookies are baked. Cool cookies on racks.

When cookies are cool, decorate as desired with frosting. To make frosting, combine powdered sugar and enough milk to make an easy-to-spread consistency. Add a few drops of food coloring as desired. Spread on cookies to decorate.

This is a holiday favorite at our house. Santa likes these cookies too.

SNICKERDOODLE COOKIES

Makes 4 dozen cookies

1 cup butter

1 1/2 cups plus 2 tablespoons sugar, divided use

2 eggs, beaten

2 3/4 cups flour

2 teaspoons baking soda

1/2 teaspoon salt

2 teaspoons cinnamon

Preheat oven to 400 degrees.

In a medium bowl with a handheld mixer, beat together butter and 1 1/2 cups sugar. Add eggs, mixing well again.

In another small bowl, combine the flour, baking soda, and salt. Gradually add the flour mixture to the butter mixture, mixing well. Mixture should be stiff.

In a small bowl, mix remaining 2 tablespoons sugar and cinnamon. Roll batter into small balls, about the size of a walnut. Roll each in sugar-cinnamon mixture.

Place cookies 2 inches apart on an ungreased cookie sheet. Flatten each cookie with a fork dipped in water, making a crisscross pattern on top. Bake 8 to 10 minutes or until lightly brown around the edges. Repeat until all dough is used.

This is a great cookie for any time or occasion.

Mrs. Thompson's Refrigerator Oatmeal Cookies

Makes about 3 dozen cookies

1 cup vegetable shortening

1 cup packed brown sugar

1 cup sugar

2 eggs, beaten

1 teaspoon vanilla

1 1/2 cups flour

1 teaspoon salt

1 teaspoon baking soda

1 teaspoon cinnamon

3 cups quick cooking oats

1/2 cup chopped pecans

In a large bowl with a handheld mixer, beat together shortening, brown sugar, and sugar until light and fluffy. Add eggs and vanilla, mixing well again.

In a medium bowl, mix together the flour, salt, soda, and cinnamon. Gradually add the flour mixture to the sugar mixture until well-combined. Stir in nuts and oats. Form dough into three log-shaped rolls, wrapping each in waxed paper. Chill overnight.

When ready to bake, preheat the oven to 350 degrees.

Slice dough 1/4" thick. Place cookies 2 inches apart on an ungreased cookie sheet and bake for about 10 minutes or until golden brown. Repeat until all dough is used.

OATMEAL RAISIN COOKIES

Makes 4 dozen cookies

3/4 cup flour

1/2 teaspoon baking soda

1 teaspoon cinnamon

1/2 teaspoon salt

1/2 cup butter, softened at room temperature

1/3 cup sugar

1/4 cup brown sugar

1 egg, beaten

1/4 teaspoon vanilla

1 1/2 cups rolled oats (not instant)

3/4 cup raisins

Preheat oven to 350 degrees.

    In a medium bowl, combine flour, baking soda, cinnamon, and salt. In a large bowl with a handheld mixer, beat together butter, sugar, and brown sugar until light and fluffy. Beat in egg and vanilla. Gradually add the dry ingredients until just combined. Stir in oats and raisins.

    Drop 2-tablespoon portions onto ungreased cookie sheets, about 2 inches apart. Bake until golden, about 8 to 10 minutes. Repeat until all dough is used.

Oatmeal Butterscotch Cookies

Makes 4 dozen cookies

3/4 cup butter, softened at room temperature

3/4 cup sugar

3/4 cup packed light brown sugar

2 eggs

1 teaspoon vanilla

1 1/4 cups flour

1 teaspoon baking soda

1/2 teaspoon salt

1/2 teaspoon cinnamon

3 cups quick-cooking oats, uncooked

1 10-ounce package butterscotch chips

Preheat oven to 375 degrees.

In a large bowl with a handheld mixer, beat together the butter, sugar, and brown sugar until well-blended. Add eggs and vanilla; blend thoroughly.

In a medium bowl, stir together flour, baking soda, salt, and cinnamon; gradually add to the butter mixture, beating until well-blended. Stir in oats and butterscotch chips; mix well.

Drop by teaspoonfuls onto ungreased cookie sheet. Bake 8 to 10 minutes or until golden brown. Cool slightly; then remove to wire rack. Repeat until all dough is used.

Goebel's Brown Sugar Cookies

Makes about 4 dozen cookies

2 eggs, beaten

2 cups packed brown sugar

1/2 cup butter, melted

1 teaspoon vanilla

3 1/2 cups flour

1 teaspoon baking powder

1 teaspoon baking soda

1/2 cup chopped pecans

1 cup Rice Krispies cereal

Preheat oven to 350 degrees.

In a large bowl, beat together eggs, brown sugar, melted butter, and vanilla.

In another large bowl, combine flour, baking powder, and baking soda. Gradually add to egg and sugar mixture until ingredients are well-blended. Stir in pecans and cereal.

Drop batter by rounded teaspoonfuls onto an ungreased cookie sheet and bake for 8 to 10 minutes. Repeat until all dough is used.

These delicious cookies were my Popo's favorite.

Weiderstein Chocolate Cookies

Makes about 4 dozen cookies

4 eggs, beaten

3 cups sugar

1 teaspoon vanilla

1 teaspoon salt

1 1/2 cups flour

1/2 box (4 ounces) Hershey's unsweetened cocoa

1 teaspoon baking powder

2 cups whole pecans

Preheat oven to 350 degrees.

In a large bowl with a handheld mixer, beat together eggs, sugar, and vanilla until light and fluffy.

In a medium bowl, combine salt, flour, cocoa, and baking powder. Gradually add dry ingredients to egg and sugar mixture until well-blended.

Drop rounded teaspoonfuls onto ungreased cookie sheet, about 2 inches apart. Press one whole pecan in center. Bake for 10 to 12 minutes. Repeat until all batter is used.

Traditional Toll House Cookies

Makes 4 dozen cookies

1 cup plus 2 tablespoons flour

1/2 teaspoon baking soda

1/2 teaspoon salt

1 teaspoon cream of tartar

1/2 cup butter, softened at room temperature

6 tablespoons sugar

6 tablespoons packed brown sugar

½ teaspoon vanilla

1 egg, beaten

1 6-ounce package semi-sweet chocolate chips

1/2 cup chopped nuts (optional)

Preheat oven to 375 degrees.

In a small bowl, combine flour, baking soda, cream of tartar, and salt; set aside.

In large bowl with a handheld mixer, beat together butter, sugar, brown sugar, and vanilla until creamy. Beat in egg.

Gradually add flour mixture; mix well. Stir in chocolate chips and nuts (if desired).

Drop by rounded teaspoonfuls onto ungreased cookie sheet, about 2 inches apart. Bake for approximately 8 to 10 minutes until lightly browned around the edges. Repeat until all dough is used.

**The addition of cream of tartar
makes this cookie deliciously crisp.**

Chocolate Peanut Butter Chip Cookies

Makes 4 dozen cookies

8 1-ounce squares semi-sweet chocolate

3 tablespoons butter

1 14-ounce can sweetened condensed milk

2 cups Bisquick

1 egg, beaten

1 teaspoon vanilla

1 cup peanut butter-flavored chips

Preheat oven to 350 degrees.

In large saucepan over low heat, combine chocolate, butter, and condensed milk. Stir and cook until chocolate is melted. Remove from heat.

Add Bisquick, egg, and vanilla; with handheld mixer, beat until smooth and well-blended. Let mixture cool to room temperature. Stir in peanut butter chips.

Drop batter by rounded teaspoonfuls onto ungreased baking sheets, about 2 inches apart. Bake 6 to 8 minutes or until tops are lightly crusted. Repeat until all dough is used.

RANGER COOKIES

Make 4 dozen cookies

1 cup butter, softened at room temperature

1 cup sugar

1 cup packed brown sugar

2 eggs, beaten

1 teaspoon vanilla

1 teaspoon baking soda

1/2 teaspoon salt

1/2 teaspoon baking powder

2 cups flour

2 cups old-fashioned rolled oats

3 cups Rice Krispies cereal

1 cup shredded coconut

1 cup chopped pecans

Preheat oven to 300 degrees.

In a large bowl with a handheld mixer, beat together the butter, sugar, and brown sugar until ingredients are creamy. Add the eggs and vanilla, mixing well.

In a medium bowl, combine flour, baking powder, salt, and baking soda. Gradually add to butter mixture. Stir in the oats, Rice Krispies, coconut, and pecans.

Drop batter by teaspoonfuls about 2 inches apart on ungreased baking sheet sprayed with cooking spray. Bake for 7 to 8 minutes or until edges are light brown. Repeat until all dough is used.

This is one of the favorites of former First Lady Laura Bush.

Desserts

Cakes

TIP

To test when a cake is done, insert wooden pick into middle of cake. When pick comes out clean, cake is done.

Banana Split Cake

Makes 8 to 10 servings

Crust

1/2 cup butter, melted

2 cups graham cracker crumbs

3 teaspoons sugar

Layers

1/2 cup butter, softened at room temperature

2 cups (16 ounces) powdered sugar

2 eggs

5 large bananas, sliced

1 20-ounce can crushed pineapple, drained

1 10-ounce tub Cool Whip, thawed

4 tablespoons chocolate syrup

2 tablespoons chopped pecans (optional)

For crust:

In a small bowl, mix together the melted butter, graham crackers, and sugar. Pat into the bottom of a 9″ x 13″ glass baking dish. Chill 1 hour in the freezer.

For cake layers:

In a medium bowl with a handheld mixer, beat the butter until light and fluffy. Add the powdered sugar and then the eggs. Mix at medium speed for 5 minutes.

Spread mixture evenly over crust. Top with the bananas and then the pineapple. Spread Cool Whip on top of the pineapple. Drizzle with the chocolate syrup. Sprinkle with pecans if desired.

Red Velvet Cake

Makes one 9″ x 13″ or one two-layer cake; 10 to 12 servings

1/2 cup butter, softened at room temperature

1 1/2 cups sugar

2 eggs

1 teaspoon vanilla

1 cup buttermilk

2 tablespoons red food coloring

2 cups flour

1/3 cup unsweetened cocoa

1 teaspoon salt

1 1/2 teaspoons baking soda

1 tablespoon white vinegar

1 16-ounce can ready-to-spread cream cheese frosting

Mini-chocolate chips for decoration, if desired

Preheat oven to 350 degrees. Grease and flour a 9″ x 13″ baking pan or two 9″ round cake pans.

In a large bowl with a handheld mixer, beat together butter and sugar. Beat in the eggs and vanilla.

In small bowl, stir together buttermilk and food coloring.

In a medium bowl, stir together flour, cocoa, and salt. Add alternately to butter and sugar mixture with buttermilk, blending well with electric mixer on medium speed.

Stir in baking soda and vinegar. Pour into prepared pans. Bake for 30 to 35 minutes or until a wooden pick inserted in center comes out clean.

Cool completely in pan on wire racks. Turn out of pan. Frost with icing. Decorate with mini-chocolate chips if desired.

Chocolate Brownie Cake

Makes one two-layer cake; 10 to 12 servings

Cake
- 2 cups sugar
- 1 cup butter, softened at room temperature
- 2 eggs, beaten
- 2 cups flour
- 1 teaspoon baking soda
- 4 tablespoons unsweetened cocoa powder
- 1/2 cup buttermilk
- 1/2 cup sour cream
- 1 teaspoon vanilla

Chocolate Buttermilk Frosting
- 1/2 cup butter, softened at room temperature
- 1/4 cup unsweetened cocoa
- 1 8-ounce package cream cheese
- 2 cups (16 ounces) powdered sugar
- 2 tablespoons buttermilk
- 1 teaspoon vanilla

For cake:

Preheat oven to 350 degrees. Grease and flour two 9″ cake pans.

In a medium bowl with a handheld mixer, beat together the butter and sugar until light and fluffy. Add the eggs and mix until combined.

In a medium bowl, combine the flour, baking soda, and cocoa.

In a small bowl, whisk together the buttermilk, sour cream, and vanilla.

With mixer on low speed, add dry ingredients, alternating with the liquid ingredients, to the butter and sugar mixture, mixing until batter is smooth.

Divide the cake batter evenly into cake pans and bake for about 30 to 35 minutes or until a pick comes out clean.

Cool and frost with chocolate buttermilk frosting.

For chocolate buttermilk frosting:

In a medium bowl with a handheld mixer, beat together butter, cocoa, and cream cheese on low setting to combine thoroughly. On high speed, beat ingredients until light and fluffy. On low speed, slowly add the powdered sugar, buttermilk, and vanilla. Beat until smooth.

To frost cake, spread icing on top of bottom layer. Top with second layer, and spread icing on top and sides of cake.

Millionaire Mousse Cake

Makes 10 to 12 servings

Cake

2/3 cup butter, softened at room temperature

1 cup heavy whipping cream

3/4 cup sugar

1 cup unsweetened cocoa

6 large eggs

2 teaspoons vanilla

1/4 teaspoon salt

1/2 cup flour

Glaze

12 ounces white chocolate

1/3 cup powdered sugar

1/4 cup vegetable shortening

For cake:

Preheat oven to 325 degrees. Grease bottom only of a 9″ springform pan.

In a 2-quart saucepan, combine butter, cream, and sugar over low heat just until butter melts. Remove from heat; stir in cocoa. Place saucepan in freezer, stirring mixture occasionally, until slightly thickened, about 15 to 20 minutes.

In a large bowl with a handheld mixer, beat together eggs, vanilla, salt, and flour at low speed until ingredients are combined. On high speed, beat until very light and fluffy, about 5 minutes. Stir about half of egg mixture into cooled chocolate mixture; then fold all of chocolate mixture into remaining egg mixture.

Pour batter into prepared pan. Bake for 55 to 60 minutes or until cake is firm in the middle. Run a knife around edge of cake to loosen from side of pan. Place cake on rack and cool cake completely in pan. Remove from pan. Pour glaze over top of cake to run down the sides.

For glaze:

In a 1-quart saucepan over very low heat, melt chocolate, sugar, and shortening.

Spread glaze over cake. Refrigerate until glaze is firm.

Momo's Chocolate Sheet Cake

Makes 10 to 15 servings

Cake

2 cups flour

2 cups sugar

1/4 teaspoon salt

1 cup butter

5 tablespoons unsweetened cocoa

1 cup boiling water

1/2 cup buttermilk

2 eggs, beaten

1 teaspoon baking soda

1 teaspoon vanilla

Icing

3/4 cup butter

5 tablespoons unsweetened cocoa

6 tablespoons milk

1 teaspoon vanilla

2 cups powdered sugar

1/2 cup finely chopped pecans

For cake:

Preheat oven to 350 degrees. Coat a 12″ x 17″ sheet cake pan with cooking spray or spread with a light coating of butter or shortening.

In a large mixing bowl, combine the flour, sugar, and salt.

In a medium saucepan, melt the butter over low heat. Add the cocoa and stir together. Add boiling water and allow mixture to boil for 30 seconds; then turn off the heat. Pour cocoa and butter mixture over flour mixture, stirring while mixture cools slightly.

In an 8-ounce measuring cup, combine the buttermilk, beaten eggs, baking soda, and vanilla. Stir buttermilk mixture into butter-chocolate mixture. Pour into prepared sheet cake pan and bake for 18 to 20 minutes or until pick comes out clean.

For icing:

While cake is baking, make the icing. In a small saucepan, melt butter over low heat. Add cocoa and stir to combine; then turn off heat. Stir in milk, vanilla, and powdered sugar until smooth. Add the pecans, mixing well.

When cake is done, pour icing over cake as soon as it comes out of oven. Cut into squares.

Aunt Meta's Heavenly Chocolate Cake

Makes one two-layer cake and 2 cups frosting

Cake	*Frosting*
2 cups sugar	1/2 cup butter
1 3/4 cups flour	2/3 cup unsweetened cocoa
3/4 cup unsweetened cocoa	3 cups powdered sugar
1 1/2 teaspoon baking powder	1/3 cup milk
1 1/2 teaspoon baking soda	1 teaspoon vanilla
1 teaspoon salt	
2 eggs, beaten	
1 cup milk	
1/2 cup vegetable oil	
2 teaspoons vanilla	
1 cup boiling water	

For cake:

Heat oven to 350 degrees. Grease and flour two 9″ round baking pans.

In a large bowl, stir together sugar, flour, cocoa, baking powder, baking soda, and salt. Using a handheld mixer, add eggs, milk, oil, and vanilla; beat at medium speed for 2 minutes. Stir in water; batter will be thin.

Pour batter evenly into prepared pans. Bake 30 to 35 minutes or until a wooden pick inserted in center comes out clean. Cool 10 minutes; remove from pans to wire racks. Cool completely.

For frosting:

In large saucepan, melt butter over low heat. Stir in cocoa. Alternately add powdered sugar and milk, beating with a handheld mixer on medium speed until smooth and easily spread. Add small amount additional milk, if needed. Stir in vanilla.

To frost cake, lightly spread top of bottom layer with frosting. Place second layer on top and spread frosting over top and sides of cake.

Chocolate Syrup Swirl Cake

Makes 8 to 10 servings

1 cup butter, softened at room temperature

2 cups sugar

2 teaspoons vanilla

3 eggs, beaten

2 3/4 cups flour

1 1/4 teaspoons baking soda, divided use

1/2 teaspoon salt

1 cup buttermilk

1 cup Hershey's chocolate syrup

Preheat oven to 350 degrees. Grease and flour 12-cup fluted Bundt pan or 10″ tube pan.

In a large bowl, beat together the butter, sugar, and vanilla with electric mixer on high speed until fluffy. Add eggs; beat well.

In a medium bowl, combine flour, 1 teaspoon baking soda, and salt; add alternately with buttermilk to butter mixture, beating until well-blended. Measure 2 cups batter and place in a small bowl; stir in syrup and remaining 1/4 teaspoon baking soda.

Pour the vanilla batter into the pan first to make bottom layer. Pour the chocolate batter over vanilla batter in pan; swirl batter with knife or ice pick.

Bake 60 to 70 minutes or until wooden pick inserted near center comes out clean. Cool 15 minutes; remove from pan to wire rack to cool completely.

MILKY WAY CAKE

Makes 8 to 10 servings

8 2-ounce Milky Way chocolate bars, cut into 1" pieces

1 cup butter, softened at room temperature, divided use

2 cups sugar

4 eggs, beaten

2 1/2 cups flour

1/4 teaspoon baking soda

1/4 teaspoon salt

1 cup buttermilk

2 teaspoons vanilla

1 cup chopped pecans

Preheat oven to 325 degrees. Coat a Bundt pan with cooking spray or spread evenly with light coating of shortening or vegetable oil.

Place pieces of candy bars in top of double boiler over hot water. Over low heat, melt candy bars and 1/2 cup butter; set aside.

In a large mixing bowl with a handheld mixer, beat together the sugar and remaining 1/2 cup butter on medium speed. Add the eggs, one at a time, mixing well until light and fluffy after the addition of each.

In a medium bowl, mix the flour, soda, and salt.

Alternately add the flour mixture and the buttermilk to sugar, butter, and eggs. Slowly add the Milky Way mixture and the pecans.

Pour batter into prepared cake pan and bake for 60 to 70 minutes or until pick inserted in center comes out clean.

Kentucky Butter Cake

Makes 12 to 15 servings

Cake

2 cups flour
2 cups sugar
1 teaspoon baking powder
1 teaspoon salt
1/2 teaspoon baking soda
1 cup buttermilk
1 cup butter, softened at room temperature
1 teaspoon vanilla
4 eggs, beaten

Butter Sauce:

3/4 cup sugar
1/3 cup butter
3 tablespoons water
2 teaspoons vanilla

For cake:

Preheat oven to 325 degrees. Grease and lightly flour a Bundt cake pan.

In a large bowl with a handheld mixer, beat together sugar, eggs, butter, and vanilla on medium, mixing well. On low speed, gradually add the flour, baking soda, baking powder, and salt. Add buttermilk slowly and beat about 3 minutes.

Pour into prepared pan and bake for 60 to 70 minutes or until wooden pick inserted in cake comes out clean.

For butter sauce:

In a medium saucepan over medium heat, combine sugar, butter, water, and vanilla. While cake is cooling, pierce holes in hot cake with an ice pick or skewer and pour butter sauce over the cake before removing it from the pan.

Rum Butter Sour Cream Cake

Makes 12 to 15 servings

Cake

3 cups flour

1 teaspoon baking powder

1/4 teaspoon baking soda

1/4 teaspoon salt

1/4 cup milk

1 tablespoon dark rum

1 cup sour cream

3/4 cup butter, softened at room temperature

2 cups sugar

2 teaspoons vanilla

3 eggs, beaten

Rum Glaze:

1/2 cup brown sugar

2 tablespoons water

2 tablespoons dark rum

2 tablespoons butter

For cake:

Preheat oven to 325 degrees. Lightly grease and flour a non-stick Bundt pan.

In a medium bowl, combine flour, baking powder, baking soda, and salt. In a small bowl, combine milk, dark rum, and sour cream.

In a large bowl with a handheld mixer, beat together butter and sugar on high speed. Add vanilla and eggs, beating until light and fluffy.

Alternately add dry ingredients and milk mixture to butter and sugar with electric mixer on low speed. When all ingredients are incorporated, mix on high until fluffy, about 3 minutes.

Pour batter into prepared Bundt pan. Bake for 60 to 70 minutes until wooden pick comes out clean when inserted into cake.

For rum glaze:

Combine brown sugar, water, and rum in a small saucepan; bring to a boil, stirring until sugar is dissolved. Add butter, stirring until butter melts.

While cake is cooling, pierce holes with ice pick or skewer and pour rum glaze over the cake before removing from pan.

Aunt Nealy's Orange Jell-O Cake

Makes 8 to 10 servings

Cake

1 box yellow cake mix

1 3-ounce box orange Jell-O

2/3 cup lukewarm water

2/3 cup cooking oil

4 small eggs, beaten

Orange Frosting

1/2 cup orange juice

1 cup powdered sugar

For cake:

Preheat oven to 325 degrees. Lightly coat a Bundt cake pan with oil or cooking spray and flour.

In a large bowl with a handheld mixer, mix together the cake mix, Jell-O, water, oil, and eggs on high for about 5 minutes or until light and fluffy.

Pour batter into prepared pan. Bake for 50 to 60 minutes or until wooden pick inserted in center comes out clean.

Cool on a rack. When cool, turn out of pan.

For orange frosting:

In a small bowl, stir together the orange juice and powdered sugar until smooth. Pour over the top of the cake.

Aunt Meta's Cheesecake

Makes 8 to 10 servings

1 box yellow cake mix, divided use

3 tablespoons butter, melted

4 eggs, beaten (divided use)

2 8-ounce packages cream cheese, softened at room temperature

1/2 cup sugar

1 1/2 cups milk

3 tablespoons lemon juice

3 teaspoons vanilla

2 21-ounce cans cherry pie filling

1 teaspoon almond flavoring

Preheat oven to 300 degrees. Lightly coat a 9″ x 13″ baking pan with oil or cooking spray.

Reserve 1 cup cake mix. In a large bowl, combine remaining cake mix with melted butter and one egg. Press into the bottom of prepared pan.

In a large bowl with a handheld mixer, combine the cream cheese and sugar on high speed, beating until smooth and sugar is dissolved. Add three eggs and the remaining cake mix. Beat one minute at medium speed. Add milk, lemon juice, and vanilla. Mixture will be thin.

Pour into pan and bake for 45 to 55 minutes. Cool completely.

In small bowl, combine cherry pie filling and almond flavoring. Spoon on top of cheesecake and refrigerate.

Chocolate Chip Cheesecake

Makes 8 to 10 servings

1 1/2 cups graham cracker crumbs

1/3 cup unsweetened cocoa

1/3 cup sugar

1/3 cup butter, melted

3 8-ounce packages cream cheese, softened at room temperature

1 14-ounce can sweetened condensed milk

3 eggs, beaten

2 teaspoons vanilla

1 cup semi-sweet mini chocolate chips, divided use

1 teaspoon flour

Preheat oven to 300 degrees.

In a small bowl, combine graham cracker crumbs, cocoa, sugar, and butter. Press evenly onto bottom of a 9" springform pan.

In large bowl with a handheld mixer, beat the cream cheese on high speed until fluffy. Gradually add sweetened milk, beating until smooth. Add eggs and vanilla, mixing well.

In small bowl, toss 1/2 cup chips with the teaspoon of flour to coat. Stir into cheese mixture. Pour into prepared pan. Sprinkle with remaining chips evenly over top.

Bake 1 hour. Turn oven off; allow cake to cool in oven for 1 hour. Remove from oven; cool to room temperature and remove from pan. Refrigerate.

Fudge Truffle Cheesecake

Makes 10 to 12 servings

1 1/2 cups vanilla wafer crumbs

1/2 cup powdered sugar

1/3 cup unsweetened cocoa

1/3 cup butter, melted

12-ounce package semi-sweet chocolate chips (2 cups)

3 8-ounce packages cream cheese, softened at room temperature

1 14-ounce can sweetened condensed milk

4 eggs, beaten

2 teaspoons vanilla

Preheat oven to 300 degrees.

In a medium bowl, stir together vanilla wafer crumbs, powdered sugar, cocoa, and melted butter. Press firmly onto bottom of a 9″ springform pan.

Place chocolate chips in microwave-safe bowl to melt. Microwave on high for 1 1/2 minutes; stir. If not completed melted, microwave on high an additional 15 seconds at a time, stirring after each heating, so that chips are just melted when stirred.

In a large bowl with a handheld mixer, beat cream cheese on high speed until fluffy. Gradually beat in sweetened milk, beating until smooth. Add melted chips, eggs, and vanilla; mix well. Pour into prepared crust.

Bake 1 hour and 5 minutes or until center is set. Remove from oven to wire rack. With knife, loosen cake from side of pan. Cool completely; remove from pan. Refrigerate several hours before serving.

Chocolate Pound Cake with Warm Chocolate Sauce

Makes two loaf cakes; 14 to 18 servings

Cake

1 cup butter, softened at room temperature

3 cups sugar

5 eggs, beaten

1 teaspoon vanilla

2 3/4 cups flour

1/2 cup unsweetened cocoa

1/2 teaspoon baking powder

1/4 teaspoon salt

1 1/4 cups whole milk

Warm chocolate sauce

12 ounces bittersweet chocolate, chopped

3/4 cup heavy whipping cream

4 tablespoons unsalted butter

2 tablespoons light corn syrup

For cake:

Preheat oven to 300 degrees. Grease and flour two 9" loaf pans.

In a large bowl with a handheld mixer, combine butter and sugar, beating at medium-high speed until fluffy. Add eggs, one at a time, beating well after each one. Add vanilla and beat again.

In a medium bowl, mix together flour, cocoa, baking powder, and salt; add to butter mixture alternately with milk, beginning and ending with the flour mixture. Beat at low speed just until blended after each addition. Pour batter into prepared pans.

Bake for 1 hour or until wooden pick inserted in center comes out clean.

For warm chocolate sauce:

In top of double boiler, combine chocolate, cream, and butter over heated water. Cook over low heat, stirring often, for 5 to 6 minutes or until melted and smooth. Stir in corn syrup until well-combined.

Remove from heat, and serve warm over cake.

Potluck Pound Cake

Makes one 10" cake

Cake

1 1/2 cups butter, softened at room temperature
1 8-ounce package cream cheese, softened at room temperature
3 cups sugar
1 teaspoon vanilla
5 eggs, beaten
3 1/4 cups flour
1/2 teaspoon baking powder
1/4 teaspoon salt

Glaze

1 cup powdered sugar
2 tablespoons heavy cream

For cake:

Preheat oven to 325 degrees. Lightly coat Bundt pan with cooking spray and flour.

In a large bowl with a handheld mixer, combine the butter and cream cheese on medium speed until creamy. Add sugar and vanilla, beating at medium speed until fluffy. Add eggs one at a time, beating well after each addition.

In a medium bowl, combine flour, baking powder, and salt. Gradually add to butter mixture, beating until combined. Spoon batter into prepared pan.

Bake for 1 hour and 15 to 20 minutes or until a wooden pick inserted in center comes out clean. Cool in pan for 10 minutes. Remove from pan and cool completely.

For glaze:

In a small bowl, combine powdered sugar and cream, whisking until smooth.
Drizzle over cooled cake.

Desserts

Pies

TIP

Test whether a pie is done by inserting a knife in the middle. Pie is done if knife comes out clean.

Homestyle Apple Pie

Makes one pie; 8 servings

1 package refrigerated pie crust

1/4 cup plus 1 tablespoon sugar, divided use

1/4 cup packed brown sugar

3 tablespoons cornstarch

1 teaspoon cinnamon

6 large Granny Smith apples, peeled, cored, and sliced

2 tablespoons heavy cream

Preheat oven to 350 degrees.

On a lightly floured surface, roll out one pie crust into a 12" circle. Fit crust into 9" deep-dish pie plate according to package directions.

In a large bowl, combine 1/4 cup sugar, brown sugar, cornstarch, and cinnamon. Add apples, tossing gently to coat. Spoon mixture into prepared crust.

On a lightly floured surface, roll out remaining pie crust. Using a pastry wheel or knife, cut into 1/2" wide strips. Arrange strips in a lattice design over apple mixture. Trim pastry strips even with pie edge. Press edges of crust together. Fold edges under, and crimp. Brush crust with cream, and sprinkle with remaining 1 tablespoon sugar.

Bake for 45 to 50 minutes or until lightly browned. Remove to a wire rack and cool at least 30 minutes before serving.

Chocolate Chess Pie

Makes one pie; 8 servings

1/2 cup butter
1 1/2 squares (1-ounce) unsweetened baking chocolate, chopped
1 cup packed brown sugar
1/2 cup sugar
2 eggs, beaten
1 tablespoon milk
1 teaspoon flour
1 teaspoon vanilla
1 9" refrigerated pie crust
Whipped cream for garnish

Preheat oven to 325 degrees.

In a small saucepan, melt butter and chocolate over low heat; set aside.

Combine sugars, eggs, milk, flour, and vanilla in a medium bowl. Gradually add chocolate mixture, beating constantly.

Pour into pie crust and bake for 40 to 45 minutes.

Let cool before serving. Garnish with whipped cream.

Grandma Lane's East Texas Buttermilk Pie

Makes one pie; 8 servings

1 1/2 cups sugar
1 tablespoon flour
3 eggs, beaten
1/2 cup butter, melted
1 teaspoon vanilla
1/2 cup buttermilk
1 9" refrigerated pie crust

Preheat oven to 375 degrees.

In a medium bowl, combine the flour and sugar. Stir in eggs. Beat in the melted butter; add vanilla, then the buttermilk, mixing well to combine.

Pour into unbaked pie shell and bake for 35 to 40 minutes or until firm in the middle.

Easy Pecan Pie

Makes one pie; 8 servings

3 eggs, beaten
1 cup light or dark corn syrup
1 cup sugar
2 tablespoons butter, melted
1 teaspoon vanilla
1 1/2 cups coarsely chopped pecans
1 9" refrigerated pie crust

Preheat oven to 350 degrees.

In a large bowl, combine all ingredients except pecans, stirring until well-blended. Stir in nuts.

Pour into unbaked pie crust. Bake for 50 to 55 minutes or until knife inserted in the middle comes out clean.

Bourbon Pecan Pie

Makes one pie; 8 servings

3 ounces bourbon
1 cup pecans, chopped
4 eggs, beaten
1 cup sugar
1 cup dark corn syrup
1/2 cup butter, melted
1 teaspoon vanilla
10 ounces chocolate chips
1 9" refrigerated pie crust

Preheat oven to 325 degrees.

In small bowl, combine bourbon and pecans; set aside.

In medium bowl, combine eggs with sugar, beating with electric mixer on low speed until smooth. Slowly add corn syrup, butter, and vanilla. Let stand for 4 minutes; add chocolate chips and the bourbon-soaked pecans.

Pour into the pie shell. Bake for 40 minutes or until center is firm.

Key Lime Pie

Makes one pie; 8 servings

3 eggs, separated

1 14-ounce can sweetened condensed milk

1/2 cup key lime juice

2 to 3 drops green food coloring, optional

1 9" graham cracker crust pie shell

¼ teaspoon cream of tartar

1/3 cup sugar

Preheat oven to 325 degrees.

In medium bowl, beat egg yolks; gradually beat in sweetened milk and lime juice. Stir in food coloring. Pour into pie crust.

Bake 30 minutes. Remove from oven. Increase oven temperature to 350 degrees.

In large bowl, beat together egg whites and cream of tartar with electric mixer on high speed until soft peaks form. Gradually beat in sugar on medium speed, 1 tablespoon at a time; beat 4 minutes or until sugar is dissolved and stiff glossy peaks form. Immediately spread meringue over hot pie, carefully sealing to edge of crust to prevent meringue from shrinking.

Bake 15 minutes. Cool 1 hour. Chill at least 3 hours.

Chocolate Buttercream Pie

Makes one pie; 8 servings

4 ounces unsweetened chocolate, broken into chunks	2 teaspoons vanilla
3/4 cup butter, softened at room temperature	4 eggs, beaten
	1 9" refrigerated pie crust, baked
1 cup sugar	Whipped cream for topping

Place chocolate in microwave-safe bowl to melt. Microwave on high for 1 minute; stir. If not completed melted, microwave on high an additional 15 seconds at a time, stirring after each heating, so that chocolate is just melted when stirred.

In small mixing bowl, beat butter with electric mixer on high speed until fluffy. Add sugar, melted chocolate, and vanilla. Beat until light and fluffy. Add eggs. Beat about 3 minutes until thick and smooth.

Pour into baked pie shell and chill. Garnish with whipped cream.

Chocolate Cream Pie

Makes one pie; 8 servings

1/4 cup unsweetened cocoa	3 cups milk
1 cup sugar	2 tablespoons butter
1/4 cup cornstarch	2 teaspoons vanilla
1/2 teaspoon salt	1 9" refrigerated pie crust, baked
4 egg yolks, beaten	Whipped cream for garnish

In a medium saucepan, blend the cocoa, sugar, cornstarch, and salt in saucepan. Combine well-beaten egg yolks with milk. Gradually add to dry ingredients and blend well. Add butter to saucepan and cook over low heat, stirring constantly, until mixture boils and thickens. Remove from heat; stir in vanilla. Cover and cool in sink with cool water.

Pour into baked pie shell. Chill. Top with whipped cream just before serving.

French Silk Chocolate Pie

Makes one pie; 8 servings

1/2 cup butter, softened at room temperature

3/4 cup sugar

1 ounce unsweetened chocolate, melted and cooled

3 tablespoons unsweetened cocoa

1 teaspoon vanilla

2 eggs, beaten

1 9" refrigerated pie crust, baked

1 cup heavy cream, well-chilled

1/4 cup powdered sugar

1 teaspoon vanilla

1 3-ounce package slivered almonds, toasted, or chocolate sprinkles (optional)

In a medium bowl with a handheld mixer, combine butter and sugar, beating on high speed until fluffy. Add chocolate, cocoa, and vanilla; beat well. Add one egg and beat for 5 minutes. Add second egg and beat additional 5 minutes.

Pour mixture into baked pie shell and chill at least 2 hours.

In a medium bowl, combine heavy cream, powdered sugar, and vanilla. Beat with a handheld mixer at high speed until stiff peaks form. Garnish pie with whipped cream mixture and toasted almonds or chocolate sprinkles.

Desserts

Others

TIP

Add a special touch to any dessert by adding a chocolate dipped strawberry. Simply select your desired number of long-stemmed strawberries, rinse, and pat dry. Melt 1 or 2 cups of semi-sweet chocolate chips in a deep microwave-safe bowl. Microwave on high for 45 seconds; stir. Repeat as needed at 15-second intervals until chips are melted. Holding strawberries by the stem, dip berries into the chocolate. Spoon the chocolate over 2/3 of the strawberry, knocking off excess chocolate. Place on a cookie sheet lined with wax paper. Refrigerate for 30 to 45 minutes.

Double Delicious Cookie Bars

Makes 24 to 36 bars

1 1/2 cups graham cracker crumbs

1/2 cup butter, melted

1 14-ounce can sweetened condensed milk

1 cup (8 ounces) semi-sweet chocolate chips

1 cup (8 ounces) peanut butter chips

Preheat oven to 350 degrees.

In a small bowl, combine graham cracker crumbs and butter; mix well. Press crumb mixture firmly on bottom of 9″ x 13″ baking pan. Pour sweetened milk evenly over crumb mixture. Layer evenly with chocolate and peanut butter chips; press chips firmly with fork.

Bake 25 to 30 minutes or until lightly browned. Cut into bars.

BROWNIE CHEESECAKE BARS

Makes 24 to 36 bars

1 1/2 cups flour

1 1/2 cups sugar

2/3 cup butter, melted

2/3 cup unsweetened cocoa

3 eggs, beaten (divided use)

1/2 cup milk

3 teaspoons vanilla, divided use

1/2 teaspoon baking powder

1 cup chopped pecans, chopped (optional)

1 8-ounce package cream cheese, softened at room temperature

2 tablespoons butter

1 tablespoon cornstarch

1 14-ounce can sweetened condensed milk

Preheat oven to 350 degrees. Lightly coat a 9″ x 13″ pan with vegetable oil or cooking spray.

In medium bowl, combine flour, sugar, melted butter, cocoa, two eggs, milk, 2 teaspoons vanilla, and baking powder, stirring until well-blended. Stir in nuts. Spread into pan.

In small bowl, combine cream cheese, 2 tablespoon butter, and cornstarch, beating with a handheld mixer on high speed until fluffy. Gradually add sweetened condensed milk, then remaining one egg and 1 teaspoon vanilla, beating until smooth. Pour over brownie batter.

Bake for 35 to 40 minutes or until lightly browned.

Cool, refrigerate; cut into bars.

Nanino Bars

Makes 24 to 36 bars

Bar

1/2 cup butter, softened at room temperature
1/2 cup sugar
5 tablespoons unsweetened cocoa
1 teaspoon vanilla
1 egg, beaten
2 cups graham cracker crumbs
1 cup shredded coconut
1/2 cup chopped pecans

Icing

1/2 cup butter, softened at room temperature
3 tablespoons milk
2 tablespoons vanilla custard mix
2 cups powdered sugar
4 squares semi-sweet chocolate
1 tablespoon butter

For bar:

Combine butter, sugar, cocoa, vanilla, and egg in the top of a double boiler over low heat. Stir well until butter is melted and mixture is consistency of thin custard.

In a small bowl, combine graham cracker crumbs, coconut, and nuts; blend well. Add to custard mixture, mixing well. Pack batter evenly in a 9″ square pan.

For icing:

In a small bowl, beat butter with electric mixer on high speed until fluffy.

In another small bowl, blend the milk with the custard mix. Add to butter. Blend in powdered sugar. Spread over bar batter and place in refrigerator for 15 minutes to harden.

In small microwave-safe bowl, cook chocolate on high heat for 15 seconds to melt. Repeat as needed until melted. Blend in butter. Spread over custard layer.

LUSCIOUS LEMON BARS

Makes 24 bars

1 cup butter, melted

1/2 cup powdered sugar

2 cups flour

4 eggs

2 cups sugar

1/2 cup flour

1/2 teaspoon baking powder

6 tablespoons lemon juice

Preheat oven to 350 degrees.

In a small bowl, combine melted butter, powdered sugar, and flour. Pat evenly into bottom of a 9″ x 13″ baking pan; bake for 15 to 20 minutes.

Meanwhile prepare the lemon layer.

In a medium bowl with a handheld mixer, beat eggs on medium speed until fluffy. Add sugar and mix well. Add flour, baking powder, and lemon juice; mix until well-blended.

Pour over cookie layer and return to the oven. Bake for 25 to 30 minutes or until set.

Cool and cut into squares.

Pecan Pie Bars

Makes 16 bars

1 box yellow cake mix, divided use

1/4 cup butter, melted

4 eggs, divided use

1/2 cup brown sugar

1 1/2 cups light corn syrup

1 teaspoon vanilla

1 cup chopped pecans

Preheat oven to 350 degrees. Grease a 9" x 13" baking pan.

Measure 2/3 cup cake mix and set aside. In a medium bowl, combine remaining cake mix, butter, and one egg. Mix until crumbly. Press in bottom of prepared baking pan. Bake until light brown, about 15 to 20 minutes.

Meanwhile in a medium bowl, combine the remaining cake mix, brown sugar, syrup, vanilla, and three eggs. Beat until well-blended.

Remove crust from oven. Pour filling over top and sprinkle with the chopped nuts. Return to oven and bake for 30 to 35 minutes.

Cool and cut into bars.

STREUSEL CARAMEL BARS

Makes 24 bars

2 cups flour

1/4 cup firmly packed light brown sugar

1 egg, lightly beaten

3/4 cup cold butter, divided use

3/4 cup chopped pecans

24 caramels, unwrapped

1 14-ounce can sweetened condensed milk

Preheat oven to 350 degrees. Grease a 9″ x 13″ baking pan.

In a large bowl, combine flour, brown sugar, and egg. Using two knives or a pastry blender, cut in 1/2 cup butter until crumbly. Stir in pecans. Reserve 2 cups crumb mixture. Press remaining crumb mixture firmly on bottom of prepared baking pan.

Bake 15 minutes.

In small saucepan over low heat, melt caramels and remaining 1/4 cup butter with sweetened milk. Pour over prepared crust. Top with reserved crumb mixture.

Bake 20 minutes or until bubbly.

Cut into bars.

Turtle Brownies

Makes 24 bars

1 14-ounce package caramels, unwrapped
2/3 cup evaporated milk, divided use
1 box German chocolate cake mix, divided use
1/2 cup butter, softened at room temperature
8 ounces semi-sweet chocolate chips
1 cup chopped pecans

Preheat oven to 350 degrees.

In a small saucepan, heat caramels and 1/3 cup evaporated milk over low heat until creamy, stirring constantly. Keep warm.

In a medium bowl, stir together cake mix, butter, and 1/3 cup evaporated milk, mixing until smooth. Pat evenly into the bottom of a 9″ x 13″ baking dish. Bake for 6 minutes.

In the following order, layer chocolate chips, nuts, and melted caramels on top of baked cake. Drop the remaining cake mix by rounded tablespoons evenly over the caramel layer, gently pressing mix into caramel layer. Bake for 20 minutes.

Let cool. Refrigerate before serving. Cut into bars.

Bananas Foster

Makes 4 servings

1/4 cup butter

1 cup brown sugar

1/2 teaspoon cinnamon

1/4 cup banana rum

1/4 cup light or dark rum

4 bananas, peeled and sliced 1/2" thick

4 scoops vanilla ice cream

In a skillet, melt the butter along with sugar and cinnamon over low heat, stirring until sugar dissolves. Stir in banana rum and bananas. When bananas soften, carefully add the light or dark rum. Continue to cook the sauce until the rum is hot; then tip the pan slightly and, if desired, ignite the rum using a long-handled click lighter. When the flames subside, lift out the bananas with a slotted spoon and place over ice cream in individual bowls. Spoon warm sauce over the top of the ice cream and serve immediately.

This is a very impressive dessert to make for a dinner party.

Chocolate Bread Pudding

Makes 6 to 8 servings

2 cups semi-sweet chocolate chips, divided use

4 eggs, lightly beaten

3/4 cups firmly packed light brown sugar

1/2 teaspoon cinnamon

1/8 teaspoon nutmeg

1 teaspoon vanilla

1/2 cup Kahlua (coffee liqueur) or brandy

2 cups milk

4 cups stale French bread cubes

Preheat oven to 350 degrees. Grease a 5-cup loaf pan.

In microwave-safe measuring cup, melt 1 cup chocolate chips in microwave on high heat for 30 seconds. Stir and repeat until all chips are melted. Set aside to cool.

In a large bowl, whisk together eggs, brown sugar, cinnamon, nutmeg, vanilla, melted chocolate, and Kahlua, mixing until smooth; when smooth, stir in milk and mix well. Stir in bread cubes and let stand for 30 minutes, stirring occasionally to make sure bread is evenly soaked.

Ladle half the bread mixture into loaf pan. Spread remaining 1 cup chocolate chips evenly on top. Ladle remaining bread mixture over chocolate chips.

Bake for about 55 minutes or until center is set.

Serve warm with cream or milk.

This is a real crowd pleaser for any outdoor summer event.

CREAMY BANANA PUDDING
Makes 6 to 8 servings

1 14-ounce can sweetened condensed milk

1 1/2 cups cold water

1 3.4-ounce box (4-serving size) instant vanilla pudding and pie mix

2 cups heavy cream, whipped to soft peaks or 1 8-ounce tub whipped topping (reserve ¼ cup)

1 12-ounce box vanilla wafers, divided use

4 bananas, sliced and dipped in lemon juice, divided use

In large bowl, stir together sweetened milk and water. Add pudding mix, beating well with a handheld mixer on medium speed. Chill 5 minutes.

Reserve 1/4 cup whipped cream. Using a spatula, fold remaining whipped cream into chilled milk and water.

Crush enough wafers to make 1/3 cup crumbs and reserve.

Spoon 1 cup of pudding mixture into 1 1/2-quart glass serving bowl. Top with 1/3 each of wafers and bananas. Repeat layering twice, ending with pudding. Top with reserved whipped cream and wafer crumbs. Chill thoroughly.

Show-Stopping Trifle

Makes 12 servings

1 3.4-ounce box (4-serving size) instant vanilla pudding and pie mix
2 1/2 cups half-and-half
12 ladyfingers
1/4 cup sherry, divided use
1 pint fresh sliced strawberries, divided use
1 cup heavy cream, whipped to soft peaks

Prepare pudding mix according to package directions, using half-and-half for milk. Set aside.

Line bottom of glass trifle bowl with ladyfingers. Drizzle with 1/8 cup sherry, sprinkle with 1/3 of the berries, and top with half of the pudding. Repeat layers, ending with berries, and top with whipped cream. May be prepared ahead and stored in refrigerator.

Quick Cobbler

Makes 6 to 8 servings

1/2 cup butter
1 1/2 cups sugar, divided use
1 cup flour
1 1/2 teaspoons baking powder
3/4 cup milk
2 cups fruit, any kind, fresh or canned (drained)

Preheat oven to 375 degrees. In 9" square baking dish, melt butter in oven while preheating. Remove from oven when butter is melted.

In medium bowl, combine 1 cup sugar, flour, baking powder, and milk. Stir and pour over butter in baking dish. Do not stir. Arrange fruit on top to cover butter. Sprinkle fruit with 1/2 cup sugar.

Bake for 30 to 40 minutes or until golden.

Terrific Toffee

Makes about 36 pieces

40 saltine crackers
1 cup butter
1 cup packed brown sugar
1 12-ounce bag semi-sweet chocolate chips
1/4 cup finely chopped pecans

Preheat oven to 400 degrees. Line 10″ x 15″ cookie sheet with foil.

Arrange saltines on foil-lined pan.

In small saucepan, melt butter and brown sugar over medium heat. Bring to a boil and cook for 3 minutes. Pour or spoon evenly over crackers.

Bake for 7 minutes, watching carefully so it does not burn.

Remove from oven and turn off oven. Immediately sprinkle with chocolate chips. Spread chips as they melt; can even place back in oven for a minute to help with spreading evenly. Lightly top with pecans.

Refrigerate until hard. Break into pieces to serve.

Store in refrigerator or freezer.

This is a great treat to have on hand during the holidays.

FANTASTIC FUDGE

Makes 48 to 54 squares

3/4 cup butter

1 5-ounce can evaporated milk

3 cups sugar

1 12-ounce package semi-sweet chocolate chips

1 7-ounce jar marshmallow crème

1 teaspoon vanilla

3/4 cups chopped pecans

Butter a 9″ x 13″ baking pan or dish.

In a heavy saucepan, melt butter over medium heat. Add milk and sugar. Bring to a boil over medium-high heat. When mixture boils to the point that you can't stir down the bubbles, cook and stir for 10 minutes.

Turn off heat, add the chocolate chips, and stir until melted. Add marshmallow crème, vanilla, and nuts. Using a spoon, beat by hand until cool.

Pour into prepared pan. Refrigerate several hours or until firm. Cut into squares.

This is another easy standby to keep handy during the holidays.

Index

A

Acorn Squash, 129
All-Time Favorite Chicken Tenders, 189
Amber's Texas-Style Steak Marinade, 99
American cheese
    Momma's Meatloaf, 149
    Oven-Baked Chili Spaghetti with Cheese, 161
American Chop Suey, 165
American Steakhouse-Style Beef, 153
anchovies
    Caesar Salad, 73
appetizers
    Asparagus Beef Roll-Ups, 46
    Caramel Corn, 55
    Deviled Eggs, 48
    Holiday Cheese Ball, 48
    Holiday Meatballs, 44
    Homemade Cheese Snack Crackers, 53
    Jalapeño Fudge, 43
    Jalapeño Poppers, 43
    Patty's Party Mix, 54
    Pepper Jack Cheese Wafers, 45
    Pepperoni Pinwheels, 49
    Pigs in a Blanket, 49
    Popcorn Balls, 52
    Praline Pecans, 52
    Puppy Chow, 54
    Rattlesnake Bites, 51
    Rum-Spiked Grilled Pineapple, 86
    Spinach Balls, 50
    Tortilla Roll-Ups, 47
    See also salads; side dishes
Apple and Horseradish-Glazed Salmon, 205
apple cider vinegar
    American Steakhouse-Style Beef, 153
    Buttermilk Dressing, 97
    Honey Mustard Dressing, 92
    Hot Bacon Dressing, 93
    Italian Salad Dressing, 97
    Maple-Vinegar Drizzle, 101
apple jelly
    Apple and Horseradish-Glazed Salmon, 205
apples
    Grandma Kattner's German Apple Cake, 257
    Homestyle Apple Pie, 267
    Opal, 90
    Weiderstein Applesauce Cake, 256
artichoke
    Hot Artichoke Dip, 29
Asian dishes
    American Chop Suey, 165
    No-Grill Teriyaki Chicken, 181
    Slow Cooker Sweet and Sour Chicken, 180
    Stir-Fry Cashew Chicken, 182
    Thai Chicken Salad with Peanut Dressing, 78
Asparagus Beef Roll-Ups, 46
Au Gratin Potatoes, 120
Aunt Meta's Cheesecake, 260
Aunt Meta's Heavenly Chocolate Cake, 250
Aunt Meta's Heavenly Holiday Salad, 84
Aunt Nealy's Orange Jell-O Cake, 259
avocados
    Avocado Mayonnaise, 106
    Chicken Tortilla Soup, 60
    Green Goddess Dressing, 95
    Guacamole, 31
    Southwest Avocado and Corn Dip, 32
    Taco Salad, 76

B

bacon
    Baked Potato Soup, 62
    Breakfast Bacon Burritos, 12
    Chicken Alfredo with Crispy Bacon, 194
    Creamed Spinach, 132

Easy Brunch Casserole, 15
Grilled Shrimp Brochettes, 202
Hot Bacon Dressing, 93
Jalapeño Poppers, 43
New Mexico Cheese and Potato Soup, 66
New Orleans Red Beans and Rice, 138
New Year's Southern-Style Black-Eyed Peas, 137
Pasta e Fagioli Soup (Italian Pasta and Bean Soup), 69
Spinach Quiche, 20
Twice-Baked Potatoes, 122
See also pork
Bahama Rum Punch, 4
Baja Pork Stir-Fry, 220
Baked Beans, 136
Baked Ham, 226
Baked Potato Soup, 62
Baked Tomatoes, 133
baking tip, 230, 244
balsamic vinegar
    Balsamic Vinaigrette, 91
    Black Bean Salsa Dip, 38
bananas
    Banana Nut Loaf, 115
    Bananas Foster, 282
    Banana Split Cake, 245
    Creamy Banana Pudding, 284
    Fruit Salad, 86
    "Pink Stuff" Salad, 85
Barbecued Pulled Pork, 219
Barbecue Sauce, 98, 99
bars, dessert
    Brownie Cheesecake Bars, 276
    Double Delicious Cookie Bars, 275
    Luscious Lemon Bars, 278
    Nanino Bars, 277
    Pecan Pie Bars, 279

Streusel Caramel Bars, 280
bay leaves
Bow Tie Pasta with Marinara Sauce, 141
Chicken Cacciatore, 171
Meat Sauce for Spaghetti, 159
New Orleans Gumbo, 70
New Orleans Red Beans and Rice, 138
New Year's Southern-Style Black-Eyed Peas, 137
beans. *See specific types*
beef
    brisket
        Smoky Marinated Beef Brisket, 153
    ground
        American Chop Suey, 165
        Chili Cheese Dip, 35
        Easy Beef Tacos, 162
        Easy Cheesy Beef Enchiladas, 164
        Holiday Meatballs, 44
        Italian Meatballs, 158
        Meat Sauce for Spaghetti, 159
        Mexican Layer Dip, 33
        Mexican Meat Pie, 163
        Momma's Meatloaf, 149
        Oven-Baked Chili Spaghetti with Cheese, 161
        Rattlesnake Bites, 51
        Taco Salad, 76
        Taco Soup with, 59
        Texas Chili, 61
    prime rib
        sauces for, 103
    ribs
        Dry-Rubbed Babyback Ribs, 226
        marinade for, 99

roast
    Asparagus Beef Roll-Ups, 46
    Crock-Pot Pot Roast, 150
    gravy for, 108
    sauces for, 103
sauces for, 101, 103
steak
    American Steakhouse-Style Beef, 153
    garnish for, 87
    Green Pepper Steak, 152
    marinade for, 98, 99
    Mongolian Beef, 157
    No-Grill Skillet Beef Tenderloin, 154
    rubs for, 100
    sauces for, 99, 107
    Slow Cooker Beef Stroganoff, 155
    Smothered Swiss Steak, 151
    Tequila-Marinated Fajitas, 156
beer
    Beer Batter Fried Seafood, 201
    Beer Marinade, 98
    Oven-Fried Halibut, 210
bell peppers
    Baja Pork Stir-Fry, 220
    Green Pepper Steak, 152
    Mexican Meat Pie, 163
    Pan-Seared Halibut with Bell Pepper Relish, 211
    Russian Dressing, 92
    Sautéed Green Beans, 134
    Spicy Chicken Chili, 64
    Tequila-Marinated Fajitas, 156
beverages
    Bahama Rum Punch, 4
    Dry Mix Spiced Tea, 3
    Easy Shower Punch, 6
    Hot Buttered Rum, 5

INDEX

Instant Hot Chocolate, 3
Kattner Strawberry Jell-O Juice Punch, 6
Pink Elephant Punch, 7
Sangria, 5
Summer Wine Cooler, 4

biscuits
Grandma Lane's Chicken and Dumplings, 67
Quick Cheese Puffs, 21

bisque
Bourbon Street Corn and Crab Bisque, 63

Bisquick
Chocolate Peanut Butter Chip Cookies, 241
French Breakfast Puffs, 22
Sausage Balls, 22

black beans
Black Bean Salsa Dip, 38
Southwest Avocado and Corn Dip, 32

Blackened Tilapia, 214

black-eyed peas
New Year's Southern-Style Black-Eyed Peas, 137
Texas Caviar, 39

blue cheese
Creamy Blue Cheese Dressing, 94
Holiday Cheese Ball, 48
Roquefort Dressing, 95

Boar's Head Brand Sweet Slice ham, 226

boiling tip, 118, 140

bourbon
Bourbon Pecan Pie, 269
Grilled Bourbon-Basted Salmon, 204
Pork Chops with Bourbon-Glazed Onions, 225

Bourbon Street Corn and Crab Bisque, 63

bow tie pasta
Bow Tie Pasta with Marinara Sauce, 141
Primavera Salad, 81

brandy
Chocolate Bread Pudding, 283
No-Grill Skillet Beef Tenderloin, 154

bread crumbs
Baked Tomatoes, 133
Chicken Cordon Bleu Casserole, 175
Chicken Divan, 176
Corn Bread Stuffing, 127
Crunchy Baked Chicken, 191
Italian Meatballs, 158
New Mexico Green Chili Macaroni and Cheese, 143
Oven-Fried Halibut, 210
Pecan-Crusted Tilapia or Trout, 213

breads
Banana Nut Loaf, 115
Cheddar Toasts, 113
Easy Pumpkin Bread, 114
French Toast, 11
Homestyle Croutons, 115
Jalapeño Hush Puppies, 111
Parmesan Garlic Twists, 113
Texas Corn Bread, 111
Zucchini Bread, 114

breakfast
Breakfast Bacon Burritos, 12
Easy Breakfast Casserole, 17
French Toast, 11
Homestyle Waffles, 11
Southwest Egg Casserole, 16
Tortilla Morning, 14
See also brunch

broccoli
Broccoli-Rice Casserole, 145
Chicken and Broccoli Alfredo, 193
Chicken Divan, 176
Classic Chicken Ring, 172

Brown Gravy, 108

brownies
Brownie Cheesecake Bars, 276
Chocolate Brownie Cake, 247
Turtle Brownies, 281

brown sugar
Baked Ham, 226
Chocolate Bread Pudding, 283
Cinnamon-Swirl Sour Cream Coffee Cake Muffins, 23
Goebel's Brown Sugar Cookies, 238
Slow Cooker Cherry-Cola Ham, 227
Thai Chicken Salad with Peanut Dressing, 78

brunch
casseroles (*See also* breakfast)
Easy Brunch Casserole, 15
Sausage Brunch Casserole, 13
Southwest Ham and Potato Chip Skillet, 18
desserts
Cinnamon Coffee Cakes, 24
Cinnamon-Swirl Sour Cream Coffee Cake Muffins, 23
quiches
Basic Ham and Cheese Quiche, 19
Spinach Quiche, 20
side dishes
Brunch Potatoes, 25
French Breakfast Puffs, 22

Quick Cheese Puffs, 21
Sausage and Egg Muffins, 21
Sausage Balls, 22
Southwest Hash Browns, 25
Buffalo Chicken Dip, 36
burritos
   Breakfast Bacon Burritos, 12
Bush, Laura, 242
butter
   Chocolate Buttercream Pie, 271
   Hot Buttered Rum, 5
   Kentucky Butter Cake, 253
   New Mexico Herb and Spice Butter, 100
   Old-Fashioned Butter Cookies, 231
   Rum Butter Sour Cream Cake, 254
   Salmon with Garlic Butter, 206
buttermilk
   All-Time Favorite Chicken Tenders, 189
   Buttermilk Dressing, 97
   Cheddar-Green Onion Muffins, 112
   Chocolate Brownie Cake, 247
   Cinnamon Coffee Cakes, 24
   Creamy Blue Cheese Dressing, 94
   Crunchy Baked Chicken, 191
   Grandma Lane's Chicken and Dumplings, 67
   Grandma Lane's East Texas Buttermilk Pie, 268
   Jalapeño Hush Puppies, 111
   Oven-Fried Chicken, 190
   Texas Corn Bread, 111
butterscotch chips
   Oatmeal Butterscotch Cookies, 237

C

cabbage
   Grandma's Old-Fashioned Cole Slaw, 82
   Momo's Cabbage Slaw, 83
cakes
   Aunt Nealy's Orange Jell-O Cake, 259
   Banana Split Cake, 245
   cheesecakes
      Aunt Meta's Cheesecake, 260
      Chocolate Chip Cheesecake, 261
      Fudge Truffle Cheesecake, 262
   chocolate
      Aunt Meta's Heavenly Chocolate Cake, 250
      Chocolate Brownie Cake, 247
      Chocolate Pound Cake with Warm Chocolate Sauce, 263
      Chocolate Syrup Swirl Cake, 251
      Milky Way Cake, 252
      Millionaire Mousse Cake, 248
      Momo's Chocolate Sheet Cake, 249
   Cinnamon Coffee Cakes, 24
   Grandma Kattner's German Apple Cake, 257
   Kentucky Butter Cake, 253
   Neiman Marcus Cake, 255
   Red Velvet Cake, 246
   Rum Butter Sour Cream Cake, 254
   tip for, 244
   Zucchini Carrot Cake, 258

cantaloupe
   Fruit Salad, 86
capers
   Lemon Chicken Picatta, 184
caramel
   Caramel Corn, 55
   Streusel Caramel Bars, 280
   Turtle Brownies, 281
carrots
   Chicken Pot Pie, 173
   Crock-Pot Pot Roast, 150
   Fried Rice, 146
   Garden Salad with Ranchy Vinaigrette, 74
   Honey Rum Carrots, 128
   Mom's Chicken Soup, 68
   Squash Stir-Fry, 130
   Thai Chicken Salad with Peanut Dressing, 78
   Zucchini Carrot Cake, 258
cashews
   Stir-Fry Cashew Chicken, 182
casseroles
   Broccoli-Rice Casserole, 145
   Chicken and Rice Casserole, 192
   Chicken Cordon Bleu Casserole, 175
   Chicken Spaghetti, 170
   Easy Breakfast Casserole, 17
   Easy Brunch Casserole, 15
   Green Bean Casserole, 134
   King Ranch Casserole, 178
   Sausage Brunch Casserole, 13
   Southwest Egg Casserole, 16
   Summer Squash Casserole, 131
   Tortilla Morning, 14
Cavender's All-Purpose Greek Seasoning, 25, 130
celery
   Chicken Pot Pie, 173

INDEX

Chicken Spaghetti, 170
Corn Bread Stuffing, 127
Mom's Chicken Soup, 68
New Orleans Gumbo, 70
Thai Chicken Salad with Peanut Dressing, 78
See also cream of celery soup

cereal
    Cornflake-Crusted Halibut with Chili-Cilantro Sauce, 212
    Crispix
        Patty's Party Mix, 54
        Puppy Chow, 54
    Rice Krispies
        Goebel's Brown Sugar Cookies, 238
        Ranger Cookies, 242

Cheddar cheese
    Baked Potato Soup, 62
    Breakfast Bacon Burritos, 12
    Buffalo Chicken Dip, 36
    Cheddar Baked Potato Slices, 121
    Cheddar-Green Onion Muffins, 112
    Cheddar Toasts, 113
    Chicken Divan, 176
    Corn Chowder Dip, 38
    Easy Brunch Casserole, 15
    Holiday Cheese Ball, 48
    Homemade Cheese Snack Crackers, 53
    Mexican Layer Dip, 33
    New Mexico Cheese and Potato Soup, 66
    Quick Cheese Puffs, 21
    Sausage Balls, 22
    Southwest Egg Casserole, 16
    Taco Salad, 76
    Texas Trash Warm Bean Dip, 34

cheese. *See specific types*

cheesecakes
    Aunt Meta's Cheesecake, 260
    Chocolate Chip Cheesecake, 261
    Fudge Truffle Cheesecake, 262

Cheez Whiz, 48

cherries
    Aunt Meta's Cheesecake, 260
    "Pink Stuff" Salad, 85

cherry cola, 227

chicken
    baked
        Chicken and Rice Casserole, 192
        Chicken Cacciatore, 171
        Chicken Cordon Bleu Casserole, 175
        Chicken Divan, 176
        Chicken Pot Pie, 173
        Classic Chicken Ring, 172
        Crunchy Baked Chicken, 191
        King Ranch Casserole, 178
        Oven-Fried Chicken, 190
        River Road Oven Chicken, 192
        Sour Cream Chicken Enchiladas, 177
        Swiss Cheese Chicken, 196
    boiled
        Chicken Spaghetti, 170
        Easy Chicken with Thin Spaghetti, 196
        Grandma Lane's Chicken and Dumplings, 67
    fried
        All-Time Favorite Chicken Tenders, 189
        Chicken Alfredo with Crispy Bacon, 194
        Chicken and Broccoli Alfredo, 193
        Chicken Florentine Pasta, 195
        Chicken Picatta with Marsala Sauce, 185
        Lemon Chicken Picatta, 184
        Maple-Mustard Glazed Chicken, 186
        Paprika Chicken, 174
        Slow Cooker Sweet and Sour Chicken, 180
        Sour Cream Chicken, 169
        Texas Spicy Chicken Breasts, 179
    gravy for, 101, 107
    grilled
        Chicken Florentine Pasta, 195
        Tequila-Glazed Grilled Chicken Breast, 183
        Warm Honey Dijon Chicken Salad, 77
    roast
        Citrus-Marinated Roast Chicken, 188
        Simple Roast Chicken, 187
    rotisserie, 28
        Thai Chicken Salad with Peanut Dressing, 78
    salad
        Classic Chicken Salad, 76
        Thai Chicken Salad with Peanut Dressing, 78
        Warm Honey Dijon Chicken Salad, 77
    shredded, cooked
        Buffalo Chicken Dip, 36
        Classic Chicken Ring, 172

Classic Chicken Salad, 76
New Mexico Cheese and
   Potato Soup, 66
soup
   Chicken Tortilla Soup, 60
   Mom's Chicken Soup, 68
stewed
   Slow Cooker Sweet and
      Sour Chicken, 180
   Spicy Chicken Chili, 64
stir-fry
   Stir-Fry Cashew Chicken,
      182
Teriyaki
   garnish for, 87
   No-Grill Teriyaki Chicken,
      181
See also cream of chicken soup
chicken broth
   Chicken Spaghetti, 170
   Chipotle Cream Sauce, 105
   Corn Bread Stuffing, 127
   Easy Chicken with Thin
      Spaghetti, 196
   King Ranch Casserole, 178
   New Mexico Cheese and Potato
      Soup, 66
   Old-Fashioned German Potato
      Salad, 80
   Pasta e Fagioli (Italian Pasta and
      Bean Soup), 69
   Roast Turkey, 197
   Slow-Roasted Pork Tenderloin
      with Cranberry Sauce, 224
   Squash Stir-Fry, 130
chicken stock
   Bourbon Street Corn and Crab
      Bisque, 63
   Texas Spicy Chicken Breasts,
      179
Chili Cheese Dip, 35

chili peppers
   chipotle
      Chipotle Cream Sauce,
         105
   green (*See also* Rotel diced
      tomatoes and green chilies)
      New Mexico Cheese and
         Potato Soup, 66
      New Mexico Green Chili
         Macaroni and Cheese,
         143
      Rattlesnake Bites, 51
      Southwest Egg Casserole, 16
      Spaghetti with Garlic, Olive
         Oil, and Chili Pepper,
         144
      Spanish Rice, 145
   poblano
      Frijoles Rancheros Beans,
         135
   red
      Mongolian Beef, 157
      Spaghetti with Garlic, Olive
         Oil, and Chili Pepper,
         144
      Tequila-Marinated Fajitas,
         156
   serrano
      Cornflake-Crusted Halibut
         with Chili-Cilantro
         Sauce, 212
   See also jalapeño peppers
Chinese dishes
   American Chop Suey, 165
   Slow Cooker Sweet and Sour
      Chicken, 180
   Stir-Fry Cashew Chicken, 182
Chipotle Cream Sauce, 105
chocolate
   baking
      Chocolate Chess Pie, 268

   bittersweet
      Chocolate Pound Cake with
         Warm Chocolate Sauce,
         263
   dipped strawberries, 274
   powder
      Instant Hot Chocolate, 3
   semi-sweet
      Bourbon Pecan Pie, 269
      Chocolate Bread Pudding,
         283
      Chocolate Chip Cheesecake,
         261
      Chocolate Peanut Butter
         Chip Cookies, 241
      Fantastic Fudge, 287
      Fudge Truffle Cheesecake,
         262
      Nanino Bars, 277
      Puppy Chow, 54
      Terrific Toffee, 286
      Traditional Toll House
         Cookies, 240
      Turtle Brownies, 281
   syrup
      Banana Split Cake, 245
      Chocolate Syrup Swirl Cake,
         251
   unsweetened
      Aunt Meta's Heavenly
         Chocolate Cake, 250
      Brownie Cheesecake Bars,
         276
      Chocolate Brownie Cake,
         247
      Chocolate Buttercream Pie,
         271
      Chocolate Chip Cheesecake,
         261
      Chocolate Cream Pie,
         271

INDEX

Chocolate Pound Cake with Warm Chocolate Sauce, 263
French Silk Chocolate Pie, 272
Fudge Truffle Cheesecake, 262
Millionaire Mousse Cake, 248
Momo's Chocolate Sheet Cake, 249
Nanino Bars, 277
Red Velvet Cake, 246
Weiderstein Chocolate Cookies, 239
  white
    Millionaire Mousse Cake, 248
chorizo sausages
  Frijoles Rancheros Beans, 135
  Southwest Hash Browns, 25
Christmas
  dishes
    Roll-Out Sugar Cookies for Santa, 233
    Sausage Brunch Casserole, 13
  gift idea, 3
cider vinegar. *See* apple cider vinegar
cilantro
  Baja Pork Stir-Fry, 220
  Black Bean Salsa Dip, 38
  Chicken Tortilla Soup, 60
  Cilantro Lime Dressing, 96
  Cornflake-Crusted Halibut with Chili-Cilantro Sauce, 212
  Cucumber Salsa, 37
  Frijoles Rancheros Beans, 135
  Guacamole, 31
  New Mexico Herb and Spice Butter, 100

Pico de Gallo, 34
Texas Caviar, 39
cinnamon
  Caramel Corn, 55
  Cinnamon Coffee Cakes, 24
  Cinnamon-Swirl Sour Cream Coffee Cake Muffins, 23
  French Breakfast Puffs, 22
  Praline Pecans, 52
  Rum-Spiked Grilled Pineapple, 86
Citrus-Marinated Roast Chicken, 188
Classic Chicken Ring, 172
Classic Chicken Salad, 76
cobbler
  Quick Cobbler, 285
cocoa. *See* chocolate
coconut
  milk
    Grilled Grouper with Soy-Ginger Glaze, 215
    Thai Chicken Salad with Peanut Dressing, 78
  shredded
    Nanino Bars, 277
    Ranger Cookies, 242
coffee liqueur, 283
cognac
  No-Grill Skillet Beef Tenderloin, 154
Colby Jack cheese
  Classic Chicken Ring, 172
  Easy Breakfast Casserole, 17
  King Ranch Casserole, 178
cookies
  Chocolate Peanut Butter Chip Cookies, 241
  Goebel's Brown Sugar Cookies, 238

Momo's No-Roll Sugar Cookies, 232
Mrs. Thompson's Refrigerator Oatmeal Cookies, 235
Oatmeal Butterscotch Cookies, 237
Oatmeal Raisin Cookies, 236
Old-Fashioned Butter Cookies, 231
Ranger Cookies, 242
Roll-Out Sugar Cookies for Santa, 233
Snickerdoodle Cookies, 234
Traditional Toll House Cookies, 240
Weiderstein Chocolate Cookies, 239
Cool Whip whipped topping
  Banana Split Cake, 245
  "Pink Stuff" Salad, 85
corn
  Bourbon Street Corn and Crab Bisque, 63
  Corn Chowder, 65
  Corn Chowder Dip, 38
  Corn Soufflé, 126
  Creamed Corn, 125
  Grandma Lane's Fried Corn, 125
  Spicy Chicken Chili, 64
corn bread
  Corn Bread Stuffing, 127
  Jalapeño Hush Puppies, 111
  Texas Corn Bread, 111
Cornflake-Crusted Halibut with Chili-Cilantro Sauce, 212
cornmeal
  Beer Batter Fried Seafood, 201
  Cheddar-Green Onion Muffins, 112
  Texas Corn Bread, 111

corn syrup
   Bourbon Pecan Pie, 269
   Caramel Corn, 55
   Chocolate Pound Cake with Warm Chocolate Sauce, 263
   Easy Pecan Pie, 269
   Popcorn Balls, 52

crab
   Bourbon Street Corn and Crab Bisque, 63
   New Orleans Gumbo, 70
   Virginia Hot Crab Dip, 30

crackers
   crushing, 110
   graham
      Banana Split Cake, 245
      Chocolate Chip Cheesecake, 261
      Double Delicious Cookie Bars, 275
      Nanino Bars, 277
   Homemade Cheese Snack Crackers, 53
   saltine
      Momma's Meatloaf, 149
      Salmon Patties, 209
      Terrific Toffee, 286

cranberries
   fresh
      Cranberry Orange Relish, 85
   juice
      Pink Elephant Punch, 7
      Sangria, 5
      Slow-Roasted Pork Tenderloin with Cranberry Sauce, 224
   sauce
      Holiday Meatballs, 44
      Slow-Roasted Pork Tenderloin with Cranberry Sauce, 224

cream
   heavy
      Chipotle Cream Sauce, 105
      Creamy Banana Pudding, 284
      French Silk Chocolate Pie, 272
      Homestyle Apple Pie, 267
      Potluck Pound Cake, 264
      Roquefort Dressing, 95
   whipping
      Aunt Meta's Heavenly Holiday Salad, 84
      Chocolate Pound Cake with Warm Chocolate Sauce, 263

cream cheese
   Asparagus Beef Roll-Ups, 46
   Aunt Meta's Cheesecake, 260
   Aunt Meta's Heavenly Holiday Salad, 84
   Brownie Cheesecake Bars, 276
   Buffalo Chicken Dip, 36
   Chicken Cordon Bleu Casserole, 175
   Chocolate Brownie Cake, 247
   Chocolate Chip Cheesecake, 261
   Creamed Spinach, 132
   Fruit Dip, 39
   Fudge Truffle Cheesecake, 262
   Game Day Cheese Dip, 36
   Holiday Cheese Ball, 48
   Jalapeño Poppers, 43
   Neiman Marcus Cake, 255
   "Pink Stuff" Salad, 85
   Potluck Pound Cake, 264
   Rattlesnake Bites, 51
   Texas Trash Warm Bean Dip, 34
   Tortilla Roll-Ups, 47

Virginia Hot Crab Dip, 30
Zucchini Carrot Cake, 258
Creamed Corn, 125
Creamed Spinach, 132
cream of celery soup
   Chicken and Rice Casserole, 192
   Chicken Spaghetti, 170
   See also celery
cream of chicken soup
   Chicken and Rice Casserole, 192
   Chicken Divan, 176
   Chicken Spaghetti, 170
   Classic Chicken Ring, 172
   Easy Cheesy Beef Enchiladas, 164
   King Ranch Casserole, 178
   Mexican Meat Pie, 163
   Sour Cream Chicken Enchiladas, 177
   Swiss Cheese Chicken, 196
   See also chicken
cream of mushroom soup
   Broccoli-Rice Casserole, 145
   Cheddar Baked Potato Slices, 121
   Chicken and Broccoli Alfredo, 193
   Chicken and Rice Casserole, 192
   Chicken Spaghetti, 170
   Crock-Pot Pot Roast, 150
   Green Bean Casserole, 134
   King Ranch Casserole, 178
   Mushroom Pork Chops, 221
   Paprika Chicken, 174
   Slow Cooker Beef Stroganoff, 155
   Summer Squash Casserole, 131
   See also mushrooms

INDEX

Creamy Banana Pudding, 284
Creamy Blue Cheese Dressing, 94
Creamy Horseradish Sauce, 103
Creole Mayonnaise, 106
crescent dinner rolls
    Classic Chicken Ring, 172
    Pepperoni Pinwheels, 49
    Pigs in a Blanket, 49
    Rattlesnake Bites, 51
    Sausage Brunch Casserole, 13
Crispix cereal
    Patty's Party Mix, 54
    Puppy Chow, 54
Crock-Pot Pot Roast, 150
croissants
    Classic Chicken Salad on, 76
croutons
    Easy Brunch Casserole, 15
    Homestyle Croutons, 115
Crunchy Baked Chicken, 191
cucumber
    Cucumber Salsa, 37
    Garden Salad with Ranchy Vinaigrette, 74
    Momo's Cucumber Salad, 83
cumin
    Mexican Meat Pie, 163
    Spice Steak Rub, 100
    Spicy Chicken Chili, 64

D

deli chicken, 28
desserts
    Bananas Foster, 282
    bars
        Brownie Cheesecake Bars, 276
        Double Delicious Cookie Bars, 275
        Luscious Lemon Bars, 278
        Nanino Bars, 277
        Pecan Pie Bars, 279
        Streusel Caramel Bars, 280
    breakfast
        Cinnamon Coffee Cakes, 24
        Cinnamon-Swirl Sour Cream Coffee Cake Muffins, 23
        French Breakfast Puffs, 22
    cakes
        Aunt Meta's Heavenly Chocolate Cake, 250
        Aunt Nealy's Orange Jell-O Cake, 259
        Banana Split Cake, 245
        Chocolate Brownie Cake, 247
        Chocolate Pound Cake with Warm Chocolate Sauce, 263
        Chocolate Syrup Swirl Cake, 251
        Grandma Kattner's German Apple Cake, 257
        Kentucky Butter Cake, 253
        Milky Way Cake, 252
        Millionaire Mousse Cake, 248
        Momo's Chocolate Sheet Cake, 249
        Neiman Marcus Cake, 255
        Red Velvet Cake, 246
        Rum Butter Sour Cream Cake, 254
        tip for, 244
        Zucchini Carrot Cake, 258
    cheesecakes
        Aunt Meta's Cheesecake, 260
        Chocolate Chip Cheesecake, 261
        Fudge Truffle Cheesecake, 262
    cookies
        Chocolate Peanut Butter Chip Cookies, 241
        Goebel's Brown Sugar Cookies, 238
        Momo's No-Roll Sugar Cookies, 232
        Mrs. Thompson's Refrigerator Oatmeal Cookies, 235
        Oatmeal Butterscotch Cookies, 237
        Oatmeal Raisin Cookies, 236
        Old-Fashioned Butter Cookies, 231
        Ranger Cookies, 242
        Roll-Out Sugar Cookies for Santa, 233
        Snickerdoodle Cookies, 234
        Traditional Toll House Cookies, 240
        Weiderstein Chocolate Cookies, 239
    Fantastic Fudge, 287
    pies
        Bourbon Pecan Pie, 269
        Chocolate Buttercream Pie, 271
        Chocolate Chess Pie, 268
        Chocolate Cream Pie, 271
        Easy Pecan Pie, 269
        French Silk Chocolate Pie, 272
        Grandma Lane's East Texas Buttermilk Pie, 268
        Homestyle Apple Pie, 267
        Key Lime Pie, 270
        tip for, 266
    pudding
        Chocolate Bread Pudding, 283

Creamy Banana Pudding, 284
Quick Cobbler, 285
Show-Stopping Trifle, 285
Terrific Toffee, 286
tips for, 244, 266, 274
Turtle Brownies, 281
Deviled Eggs, 48
Dijon mustard
Black Bean Salsa Dip, 38
Hot Bacon Dressing, 93
Spicy Chicken Chili, 64
Vinaigrette, 91
Warm Honey Dijon Chicken Salad, 77
See also mustard
Dijonnaise, 210
dill
Buttermilk Dressing, 97
dinner rolls. *See* crescent dinner rolls
dips
Black Bean Salsa Dip, 38
Buffalo Chicken Dip, 36
Chili Cheese Dip, 35
Corn Chowder Dip, 38
Cucumber Salsa, 37
Game Day Cheese Dip, 36
Guacamole, 31
Hot Artichoke Dip, 29
Mexican Layer Dip, 33
Pico de Gallo, 34
Southwest Avocado and Corn Dip, 32
Spinach Dip, 29
Texas Caviar, 39
Texas Trash Warm Bean Dip, 34
Virginia Hot Crab Dip, 30
ditalini pasta
Pasta e Fagioli Soup (Italian Pasta and Bean Soup), 69

Double Delicious Cookie Bars, 275
dressings. *See* salad dressing
drinks. *See* beverages
Dry-Rubbed Babyback Ribs, 226
Dutch oven cooking
Mom's Chicken Soup, 68
New Orleans Red Beans and Rice, 138
Pasta e Fagioli Soup (Italian Pasta and Bean Soup), 69

E
Easter dishes
Baked Ham, 226
Deviled Eggs, 48
Easy Beef Tacos, 162
Easy Breakfast Casserole, 17
Easy Brunch Casserole, 15
Easy Cheesy Beef Enchiladas, 164
Easy Chicken with Thin Spaghetti, 196
Easy Pecan Pie, 269
Easy Pumpkin Bread, 114
Easy Shower Punch, 6
egg noodles
Mom's Chicken Soup, 68
Paprika Chicken, 174
Slow Cooker Beef Stroganoff, 155
eggs
Breakfast Bacon Burritos, 12
Caesar Salad, 73
Chocolate Pound Cake with Warm Chocolate Sauce, 263
Cinnamon-Swirl Sour Cream Coffee Cake Muffins, 23
Corn Bread Stuffing, 127
Deviled Eggs, 48
Easy Breakfast Casserole, 17
Easy Brunch Casserole, 15

French Toast, 11
hard-boiled, 72
Homestyle Waffles, 11
Italian Meatballs, 158
Patty's Potato Salad, 79
Perfect Hollandaise Sauce, 102
quiches, 19, 20
Sausage and Egg Muffins, 21
Sausage Brunch Casserole, 13
Southwest Egg Casserole, 16
Southwest Ham and Potato Chip Skillet, 18
elbow macaroni
American Chop Suey, 165
Macaroni and Cheese, 142
Macaroni Salad, 82
New Mexico Green Chili Macaroni and Cheese, 143
Pasta e Fagioli Soup (Italian Pasta and Bean Soup), 69
enchiladas
Easy Cheesy Beef Enchiladas, 164
Sour Cream Chicken Enchiladas, 177
equipment, basic, xiii

F
Fantastic Fudge, 287
fettuccine
Fettuccine Alfredo, 142
fish. *See* seafood
flower arrangements, 10, 168
food processor, use of, 58
French Breakfast Puffs, 22
French Silk Chocolate Pie, 272
French Toast, 11
fried chicken. *See under* chicken
Fried Rice, 146
Frijoles Rancheros Beans, 135
Fruit Dip, 39

INDEX

fruit juice beverages, 4–7
Fruit Salad, 86
fudge
   Fantastic Fudge, 287
   Fudge Truffle Cheesecake, 262
   Jalapeño Fudge, 43

G

Game Day Cheese Dip, 36
Garden Salad with Ranchy Vinaigrette, 74
garlic
   Garlicky Grilled Shrimp, 204
   Honey-Garlic Pork Chops, 222
   Pork Medallions with Lemon-Garlic Sauce, 223
garnishes
   for beverages, 4, 7
   for brunch, 14
   for desserts, 268, 271, 272
   for main dishes, 87, 156, 162
   for salads, 76, 84, 86
   for side dishes, 138, 142
   for soup, 60, 62, 64, 65, 66, 69
Gebhardt chili powder
   in main dishes, 161, 164, 177
   in soups, 59, 61, 64
gelatin
   Jell-O
      Aunt Nealy's Orange Jell-O Cake, 259
      Kattner Strawberry Jell-O Juice Punch, 6
   lime-flavored
      Aunt Meta's Heavenly Holiday Salad, 84
      7 Up Salad, 84
"get well soup," 68
ginger ale
   Easy Shower Punch, 6
   Pink Elephant Punch, 7

ginger root
   Cilantro Lime Dressing, 96
   Grilled Grouper with Soy-Ginger Glaze, 215
   Mongolian Beef, 157
   Slow Cooker Sweet and Sour Chicken, 180
   Stir-Fry Cashew Chicken, 182
Goebel's Brown Sugar Cookies, 238
Good Seasons Italian Dressing and Recipe Mix, 32
Good Seasons Zesty Italian Dressing and Recipe Mix, 32
graham crackers
   Banana Split Cake, 245
   Chocolate Chip Cheesecake, 261
   Double Delicious Cookie Bars, 275
   Nanino Bars, 277
Grandma Kattner's German Apple Cake, 257
Grandma Lane's Chicken and Dumplings, 67
Grandma Lane's East Texas Buttermilk Pie, 268
Grandma Lane's Fried Corn, 125
Grandma's Old-Fashioned Cole Slaw, 82
grapes
   frozen, 2
   Fruit Salad, 86
gravies
   Brown Gravy, 108
   Crock-Pot Pot Roast, 150
   Smothered Swiss Steak, 151
   White Cream Gravy, 107
great northern beans
   Spicy Chicken Chili, 64

green beans
   Green Bean Casserole, 134
   Sautéed Green Beans, 134
green bell peppers. *See* bell peppers
green chili peppers. *See under* chili peppers
Green Goddess Dressing, 95
green onions. *See under* onions
Green Pepper Steak, 152
Grilled Bourbon-Basted Salmon, 204
Grilled Grouper with Soy-Ginger Glaze, 215
Grilled Salmon, 208
Grilled Shrimp Brochettes, 202
ground beef. *See under* beef
grouper
   Grilled Grouper with Soy-Ginger Glaze, 215
Gruyère cheese
   Basic Ham and Cheese Quiche, 19
   New Mexico Green Chili Macaroni and Cheese, 143
guacamole
   as ingredient, 14, 33
   recipe for, 31

H

halibut
   Cornflake-Crusted Halibut with Chili-Cilantro Sauce, 212
   Oven-Fried Halibut, 210
   Pan-Seared Halibut with Bell Pepper Relish, 211
Halloween soup, 59
ham
   Baked Ham, 226
   Basic Ham and Cheese Quiche, 19

Easy Breakfast Casserole, 17
Slow Cooker Cherry-Cola Ham, 227
Southwest Ham and Potato Chip Skillet, 18
See also pork
hash browns
    Breakfast Bacon Burritos, 12
    Southwest Egg Casserole, 16
    Southwest Hash Browns, 25
Hawaiian sweet round bread, 29
herbs. *See specific ones*
Hershey's
    chocolate syrup, 251
    unsweetened cocoa, 239
    See also chocolate
Hidden Valley Ranch Salad Dressing and Seasoning Mix, 59, 74, 121
Holiday Cheese Ball, 48
Holiday Meatballs, 44
Homemade Cheese Snack Crackers, 53
Homemade Mashed Potatoes, 119
Homestyle Apple Pie, 267
Homestyle Croutons, 115
honey
    Beer Marinade, 98
    Cilantro Lime Dressing, 96
    Citrus-Marinated Roast Chicken, 188
    Fruit Salad, 86
    Grilled Grouper with Soy-Ginger Glaze, 215
    Honey-Garlic Pork Chops, 222
    Honey Mustard Dressing, 92
    Honey Rum Carrots, 128
    Pan-Roasted Salmon, 207
    Praline Pecans, 52
    Tequila-Glazed Grilled Chicken Breast, 183
    Warm Honey Dijon Chicken Salad, 77
honey mustard
    Chipotle Cream Sauce, 105
    Honey Mustard Dressing, 92
    Hot Pepper Jelly Dipping Sauce, 105
    See also mustard
horseradish
    Apple and Horseradish-Glazed Salmon, 205
    Creamy Horseradish Sauce, 103
    Hot Pepper Jelly Dipping Sauce, 105
    Seafood Cocktail Sauce, 104
Hot Artichoke Dip, 29
Hot Bacon Dressing, 93
Hot Buttered Rum, 5
Hot Chocolate, 3
Hot Pepper Jelly Dipping Sauce, 105
hot pepper sauce (Tabasco)
    Avocado Mayonnaise, 106
    Remoulade Sauce, 103
    Stir-Fry Cashew Chicken, 182
hydrangeas, 10

I

iceberg lettuce
    Garden Salad with Ranchy Vinaigrette, 74
    Taco Salad, 76
Instant Hot Chocolate, 3
Italian dishes
    Chicken Alfredo with Crispy Bacon, 194
    Chicken and Broccoli Alfredo, 193
    Chicken Cacciatore, 171
    Chicken Florentine Pasta, 195
    Chicken Picatta with Marsala Sauce, 185
    Fettuccine Alfredo, 142
    Italian Meatballs, 158
    Lemon Chicken Picatta, 184
    Pasta e Fagioli (Italian Pasta and Bean) Soup, 69
Italian Salad Dressing, 97

J

jalapeño peppers
    Black Bean Salsa Dip, 38
    Chicken Tortilla Soup, 60
    Cilantro Lime Dressing, 96
    Corn Chowder Dip, 38
    Cucumber Salsa, 37
    Grilled Shrimp Brochettes, 202
    Guacamole, 31
    Jalapeño Fudge, 43
    Jalapeño Hush Puppies, 111
    Jalapeño Poppers, 43
    New Year's Southern-Style Black-Eyed Peas, 137
    Pico de Gallo, 34
    Rattlesnake Bites, 51
    Spicy Chicken Chili, 64
    Tequila-Marinated Fajitas, 156
    Texas Spicy Chicken Breasts, 179
    Tortilla Roll-Ups, 47
    See also chili peppers
Japanese dishes
    No-Grill Teriyaki Chicken, 181
Jell-O
    Aunt Nealy's Orange Jell-O Cake, 259
    Kattner Strawberry Jell-O Juice Punch, 6
    See also gelatin

INDEX

jelly
  apple
    Apple and Horseradish-Glazed Salmon, 205
  cranberry
    Holiday Meatballs, 44
  grape
    Slow-Roasted Port Tenderloin with Cranberry Sauce, 224
  hot pepper
    Hot Pepper Jelly Dipping Sauce, 105

K
Kahlua (coffee liqueur), 283
Kattner Strawberry Jell-O Juice Punch, 6
Kentucky Butter Cake, 253
Key Lime Pie, 270
kidney beans
  New Orleans Red Beans and Rice, 138
  Pasta e Fagioli Soup (Italian Pasta and Bean Soup), 69
King Ranch Casserole, 178
kitchen essentials, xiii, 218
Knorr Vegetable Recipe Mix, 29
Kraft Roka blue cheese spread, 48

L
ladyfingers
  Show-Stopping Trifle, 285
lamb, sauces for, 101
lasagna noodles
  Lasagna, 160
Lawry's seasoned salt, 54, 132
lemonade drinks, 3, 6
lemons
  Citrus-Marinated Roast Chicken, 188
  Grilled Lobster Tails, 201
  Lemon Chicken Picatta, 184
  Luscious Lemon Bars, 278
  Pork Medallions with Lemon-Garlic Sauce, 223
lettuce
  Boston
    Strawberry Romaine Salad, 75
  iceberg
    Garden Salad with Ranchy Vinaigrette, 74
    Taco Salad, 76
  romaine
    Caesar Salad, 73
    Strawberry Romaine Salad, 75
    Thai Chicken Salad with Peanut Dressing, 78
limes
  Cilantro Lime Dressing, 96
  Frijoles Rancheros Beans, 135
  Fruit Salad, 86
  Guacamole, 31
  Key Lime Pie, 270
  New Mexico Herb and Spice Butter, 100
  Sangria, 5
  Summer Wine Cooler, 4
  Tequila-Glazed Grilled Chicken Breast, 183
  Tequila-Marinated Fajitas, 156
  Texas Caviar, 39
  Tortilla Roll-Ups, 47
linguine
  Chicken and Broccoli Alfredo, 193
  Chicken Florentine Pasta, 195
  Lemon Chicken Picatta, 184
  Lipton Beefy Mushroom Soup Mix, 150, 155
Lipton Onion Soup and Dip Mix, 150, 155
Liquid Smoke, 153
lobster
  Grilled Lobster Tails, 201
Luscious Lemon Bars, 278

M
macaroni, elbow
  American Chop Suey, 165
  Macaroni and Cheese, 142
  Macaroni Salad, 82
  New Mexico Green Chili Macaroni and Cheese, 143
  Pasta e Fagioli Soup (Italian Pasta and Bean Soup), 69
maple syrup
  Balsamic Vinaigrette, 91
  French Toast, 11
  Maple-Mustard Glazed Chicken, 186
  Maple-Vinegar Drizzle, 101
marinades
  Amber's Texas-Style Steak Marinade, 99
  Beer Marinade, 98
  See also sauces
Marsala wine
  Chicken Picatta with Marsala Sauce, 185
marshmallows
  crème
    Fantastic Fudge, 287
    Fruit Dip, 39
  miniature
    "Pink Stuff" Salad, 85
measurement conversions, xiv
meat
  drippings for gravy, 107, 108
  sauces for, 101, 103
  See also specific types

meatballs
    Holiday Meatballs, 44
    Italian Meatballs, 158
    sauce for, 159
    Sausage Balls, 22
Meat Sauce for Spaghetti, 159
melons
    cantaloupe
        Fruit Salad, 86
    watermelon
        Fruit Salad, 86
Mexican dishes
    Mexican Layer Dip, 33
    Mexican Meat Pie, 163
    Mexicorn, 14, 32
    See also Tex-Mex dishes
milk, evaporated, 287
milk, sweetened condensed. *See* sweetened condensed milk
Milky Way Cake, 252
Millionaire Mousse Cake, 248
mint
    Fruit Salad, 86
Miracle Whip salad dressing
    Deviled Eggs, 48
    Macaroni Salad, 82
    Patty's Potato Salad, 79
    Tuna Salad, 78
molasses
    Barbecue Sauce, 98
Momma's Meatloaf, 149
Momo's Cabbage Slaw, 83
Momo's Chocolate Sheet Cake, 249
Momo's Cucumber Salad, 83
Momo's No-Roll Sugar Cookies, 232
Mom's Chicken Soup, 68
Mongolian Beef, 157
Monterey Jack cheese
    Chicken Tortilla Soup, 60
    Grilled Shrimp Brochettes, 202
    Sausage Brunch Casserole, 13
    Sour Cream Chicken Enchiladas, 177
    Spinach Quiche, 19
    Texas Trash Warm Bean Dip, 34
Mozzarella cheese
    Lasagna, 160
    Pepperoni Pinwheels, 49
Mrs. Thompson's Refrigerator Oatmeal Cookies, 235
muffins
    Cheddar-Green Onion muffins, 112
    Cinnamon-Swirl Sour Cream Coffee Cake Muffins, 23
    French Breakfast Puffs, 22
    Sausage and Egg Muffins, 21
    Texas Corn Bread, 111
Mushroom Pork Chops, 221
mushrooms
    Chicken Picatta with Marsala Sauce, 185
    Easy Chicken with Thin Spaghetti, 196
    Slow Cooker Beef Stroganoff, 155
    Wine Mushroom Sauce, 101
    See also cream of mushroom soup
mustard
    Creole
        Tartar Sauce, 104
    dry
        Grandma's Old-Fashioned Cole Slaw, 82
        New Mexico Cheese and Potato Soup, 66
        Old-Fashioned German Potato Salad, 80
        Pan-Roasted Salmon, 207
        Poppy Seed Dressing, 94
        Slow Cooker Cherry-Cola Ham, 227
        Southwest Egg Casserole, 16
        Virginia Hot Crab Dip, 30
    Honey Mustard Dressing, 92
    prepared
        Caesar Salad, 73
        Easy Brunch Casserole, 15
    stone-ground
        Maple-Mustard Glazed Chicken, 186
    whole-grain
        Pigs in a Blanket, 49
    yellow
        Baked Beans, 136
        Barbecue Sauce, 98
        Momo's Cabbage Slaw, 83
    See also Dijon mustard; honey mustard

N

Nanino Bars, 277
Neiman Marcus Cake, 255
New Mexico Cheese and Potato Soup, 66
New Mexico Green Chili Macaroni and Cheese, 143
New Mexico Herb and Spice Butter, 100
New Orleans Gumbo, 70
New Orleans Red Beans and Rice, 138
New Orleans-Style Barbecued Shrimp, 203
New Year's Southern-Style Black-Eyed Peas, 137
New York strip steaks, marinade for, 98, 99

INDEX

No-Grill Skillet Beef Tenderloin, 154
No-Grill Teriyaki Chicken, 181
nuts. *See specific types*

O

oatmeal
    Mrs. Thompson's Refrigerator Oatmeal Cookies, 235
    Oatmeal Butterscotch Cookies, 237
    Oatmeal Raisin Cookies, 236
oats, rolled
    Ranger Cookies, 242
Old Bay seasoning, 189
Old-Fashioned Butter Cookies, 231
Old-Fashioned German Potato Salad, 80
onions
    green
        Cheddar-Green Onion Muffins, 112
        Holiday Cheese Ball, 48
        Lemon Chicken Picatta, 184
        New Mexico Cheese and Potato Soup, 66
        New Orleans-Style Barbecued Shrimp, 203
    red
        Baja Pork Stir-Fry, 220
        Beer Marinade, 98
        Brunch Potatoes, 25
        Momo's Cucumber Salad, 83
        Squash Stir-Fry, 130
        Southwest Hash Browns, 25
        Taco Soup, 59
    white
        New Mexico Cheese and Potato Soup, 66
    yellow
        American Chop Suey, 165
        Chicken Cacciatore, 171
        Frijoles Rancheros Beans, 135
        Holiday Meatballs, 44
        Italian Meatballs, 158
        Meat Sauce for Spaghetti, 159
        Momma's Meatloaf, 149
        Momo's Cabbage Slaw, 83
        New Orleans Gumbo, 70
        Pork Chops with Bourbon-Glazed Onions, 225
        Simple Roast Chicken, 187
        Smothered Swiss Steak, 151
        Sour Cream Chicken, 169
        Spicy Chicken Chili, 64
        Tequila-Marinated Fajitas, 156
oranges
    Citrus-Marinated Roast Chicken, 188
    juice
        Aunt Nealy's Orange Jell-O Cake, 259
        Bahama Rum Punch, 4
        Cranberry Orange Relish, 85
        Sangria, 5
        Slow Cooker Sweet and Sour Chicken, 180
        Southern Comfort Sweet Potatoes, 124
    Sangria, 5
Oven-Baked Chili Spaghetti with Cheese, 161
Oven-Fried Chicken, 190
Oven-Fried Halibut, 210

P

pancetta
    Pasta e Fagioli Soup (Italian Pasta and Bean Soup), 69
panko bread crumbs
    Chicken Cordon Bleu Casserole, 175
    Oven-Fried Halibut, 210
    Pecan-Crusted Tilapia or Trout, 213
Pan-Roasted Salmon, 207
Pan-Seared Halibut with Bell Pepper Relish, 211
paprika
    Spice Steak Rub, 100
Paprika Chicken, 174
Parmesan cheese
    Caesar Salad, 73
    Chicken Florentine Pasta, 195
    Easy Chicken with Thin Spaghetti, 196
    Fettuccine Alfredo, 142
    Hot Artichoke Dip, 29
    Italian Meatballs, 158
    Lasagna, 160
    Parmesan Garlic Twists, 113
    Quick Cheese Puffs, 21
    Spinach Balls, 50
    Virginia Hot Crab Dip, 30
Parmesan Garlic Twists, 113
parsley, fresh
    Basic Ham and Cheese Quiche, 19
    Lemon Chicken Picatta, 184
    Spaghetti with Garlic, Olive Oil, and Chili Pepper, 144
    Vinaigrette, 91
pasta
    boiling tip, 140
    See also specific types

Pasta e Fagioli Soup (Italian Pasta and Bean Soup), 69
Patty's Party Mix, 54
Patty's Potato Salad, 79
peaches
    Red Hot Peaches, 87
peanut butter
    Puppy Chow, 54
    Thai Chicken Salad with Peanut Dressing, 78
peanut butter chips
    Chocolate Peanut Butter Chip Cookies, 241
    Double Delicious Cookie Bars, 275
pecans
    Aunt Meta's Heavenly Holiday Salad, 84
    Bourbon Pecan Pie, 269
    Brownie Cheesecake Bars, 276
    Cinnamon Coffee Cakes, 24
    Cinnamon-Swirl Sour Cream Coffee Cake Muffins, 23
    Easy Pecan Pie, 269
    Fantastic Fudge, 287
    Holiday Cheese Ball, 48
    Milky Way Cake, 252
    Pecan-Crusted Tilapia or Trout, 213
    Pecan Pie Bars, 279
    Praline Pecans, 52
    Ranger Cookies, 242
    Strawberry Romaine Salad, 75
    Streusel Caramel Bars, 280
    Sweet Potato Crunch, 123
    Terrific Toffee, 286
    Turtle Brownies, 281
    Weiderstein Chocolate Cookies, 239

penne
    Chicken Cordon Bleu Casserole, 175
Pepper Jack cheese
    Game Day Cheese Dip, 36
    New Mexico Cheese and Potato Soup, 66
    Pepper Jack Cheese Wafers, 45
pepperoni
    Pepperoni Pinwheels, 49
peppers. *See specific types*
Perfect Hollandaise Sauce, 102
Pico de Gallo, 34
pies
    Bourbon Pecan Pie, 269
    Chicken Pot Pie, 173
    Chocolate Buttercream Pie, 271
    Chocolate Chess Pie, 268
    Chocolate Cream Pie, 271
    Easy Pecan Pie, 269
    French Silk Chocolate Pie, 272
    Grandma Lane's East Texas Buttermilk Pie, 268
    Homestyle Apple Pie, 267
    Key Lime Pie, 270
    tip for, 266
    See also quiches
Pigs in a Blanket, 49
pineapples
    crushed
        Aunt Meta's Heavenly Holiday Salad, 84
        Baked Ham, 226
        Banana Split Cake, 245
        "Pink Stuff" Salad, 85
        7 Up Salad, 84
    juice
        American Steakhouse-Style Beef, 153
        Aunt Meta's Heavenly Holiday Salad, 84

Bahama Rum Punch, 4
Kattner Strawberry Jell-O Juice Punch, 6
Pink Elephant Punch, 7
Slow Cooker Sweet and Sour Chicken, 180
Tequila-Glazed Grilled Chicken Breast, 183
    whole, peeled
        Rum-Spiked Grilled Pineapple, 86
Pink Elephant Punch, 7
"Pink Stuff" Salad, 85
pinto beans, 61
    Baked Beans, 136
    Frijoles Rancheros Beans, 135
    Mexican Meat Pie, 163
Pizza Sauce, 107
poblano chili pepper
    Frijoles Rancheros Beans, 135
popcorn
    Caramel Corn, 55
    Popcorn Balls, 52
poppy seeds
    Poppy Seed Dressing, 94
pork
    barbecue
        Barbecued Pulled Pork, 219
    chops
        Honey-Garlic Pork Chops, 222
        Mushroom Pork Chops, 221
        Pork Chops with Bourbon-Glazed Onions, 225
        Pork Medallions with Lemon-Garlic Sauce, 223
    ground
        Holiday Meatballs, 44
        Italian Meatballs, 158
    sauces for, 101

INDEX

sausage
    Sausage and Egg Muffins, 21
    Sausage Balls, 22
    Southwest Egg Casserole, 16
    Tortilla Morning, 14
    Slow-Roasted Pork Tenderloin with Cranberry Sauce, 224
    See also bacon; ham
potato chips
    Southwest Ham and Potato Chip Skillet, 18
potatoes, white
    Au Gratin Potatoes, 120
    Baked Potato Soup, 62
    boiled, 72
    Breakfast Bacon Burritos with, 12
    in Crock-Pot Pot Roast, 150
    Homemade Mashed Potatoes, 119
    New Mexico Cheese and Potato Soup, 66
    Old-Fashioned German Potato Salad, 80
    Patty's Potato Salad, 79
    Ranch Fries, 121
    in Southwest Egg Casserole, 16
    Southwest Hash Browns, 25
    Twice-Baked Potatoes, 122
Potluck Pound Cake, 264
poultry. *See* chicken; turkey
powdered sugar
    Aunt Meta's Heavenly Chocolate Cake, 250
    Aunt Nealy's Orange Jell-O Cake, 259
    Banana Split Cake, 245
    Chocolate Brownie Cake, 247
    Cinnamon-Swirl Sour Cream Coffee Cake Muffins, 23
    French Toast, 11
    Grandma Kattner's German Apple Cake, 257
    Instant Hot Chocolate, 3
    Momo's Chocolate Sheet Cake, 249
    Nanino Bars, 277
    Neiman Marcus Cake, 255
    Potluck Pound Cake, 264
    Puppy Chow, 54
    Roll-Out Sugar Cookies for Santa, 233
    Zucchini Carrot Cake, 258
Praline Pecans, 52
pretzels, 54
Primavera Salad, 81
prime rib. *See under* beef
pudding mix
    Show-Stopping Trifle, 285
puddings
    Chocolate Bread Pudding, 283
    Creamy Banana Pudding, 284
pumpkin
    Easy Pumpkin Bread, 114
Puppy Chow, 54

Q

quiches
    Basic Ham and Cheese Quiche, 19
    Spinach Quiche, 20
Quick Cheese Puffs, 21
Quick Cobbler, 285

R

radishes
    flowers, 42
    Warm Honey Dijon Chicken Salad, 77
raisins
    Oatmeal Raisin Cookies, 236
Ranch Fries, 121
ranch-style beans
    Taco Salad, 76
Ranger Cookies, 242
Rattlesnake Bites, 51
Red Hots (cinnamon candy)
    Red Hot Peaches, 87
Red Velvet Cake, 246
red wine vinegar
    Cucumber Salsa, 37
    Southwest Avocado and Corn Dip, 32
    Strawberry Romaine Salad, 75
    Vinaigrette, 91
refried beans
    Texas Trash Warm Bean Dip, 34
relishes
    Cranberry Orange Relish, 85
Remoulade Sauce, 103
rice
    Broccoli Rice Casserole, 145
    Chicken and Rice Casserole, 192
    Chicken Cacciatore, 171
    Chicken Divan, 176
    Fried Rice, 146
    Mushroom Pork Chops, 221
    New Orleans Gumbo, 70
Rice Krispies cereal
    Goebel's Brown Sugar Cookies, 238
    Ranger Cookies, 242
Ricotta cheese
    Lasagna, 160
Ritz crackers, 131
River Road Oven Chicken, 192
roast beef. *See under* beef
Roast Turkey, 197
Roll-Out Sugar Cookies for Santa, 233

romaine lettuce
    Caesar Salad, 73
    Strawberry Romaine Salad, 75
    Thai Chicken Salad with Peanut Dressing, 78
Romano cheese
    Baked Tomatoes, 133
Roquefort Dressing, 95
Rotel diced tomatoes and green chilies
    Chicken Tortilla Soup, 60
    Chili Cheese Dip, 35
    Easy Cheesy Beef Enchiladas, 164
    King Ranch Casserole, 178
    Mexican Meat Pie, 163
    Sour Cream Chicken Enchiladas, 177
    Taco Soup, 59
    Texas Chili, 61
rotisserie chicken, 28
    Thai Chicken Salad with Peanut Dressing, 78
round steaks
    marinade for, 98
rubs
    Dry-Rubbed Babyback Ribs, 226
    New Mexico Herb and Spice Butter, 100
    Spice Steak Rub, 100
rum
    Bananas Foster, 282
    drinks with, 4, 5
    extract as ingredient, 52
    Honey Rum Carrots, 128
    Hot Buttered Rum, 5
    Rum Butter Sour Cream Cake, 254
    Rum-Spiked Grilled Pineapple, 86
Russian Dressing, 92

S

salad dressing
    Balsamic Vinaigrette, 91
    Buttermilk Dressing, 97
    Cilantro Lime Dressing, 96
    Creamy Blue Cheese Dressing, 94
    Green Goddess Dressing, 95
    Honey Mustard Dressing, 92
    Hot Bacon Dressing, 93
    Italian Salad Dressing, 97
    Poppy Seed Dressing, 94
    Roquefort Dressing, 95
    Russian Dressing, 92
    Vinaigrette, 91
salads
    Aunt Meta's Heavenly Holiday Salad, 84
    Caesar Salad, 73
    Classic Chicken Salad, 76
    Cranberry Orange Relish, 85
    Fruit Salad, 86
    Garden Salad with Ranchy Vinaigrette, 74
    Grandma's Old-Fashioned Cole Slaw, 82
    Macaroni Salad, 82
    Momo's Cabbage Slaw, 83
    Momo's Cucumber Salad, 83
    Old-Fashioned German Potato Salad, 80
    Patty's Potato Salad, 79
    "Pink Stuff" Salad, 85
    Primavera Salad, 81
    7 Up Salad, 84
    Strawberry Romaine Salad, 75
    Taco Salad, 76
    Thai Chicken Salad with Peanut Dressing, 78
    Tuna Salad, 78
    Warm Honey Dijon Chicken Salad, 77
salmon
    Apple and Horseradish-Glazed Salmon, 205
    Grilled Bourbon-Basted Salmon, 204
    Grilled Salmon, 208
    Pan-Roasted Salmon, 207
    Salmon Patties, 209
    Salmon with Garlic Butter, 206
    sauces for, 105
salsa
    Black Bean Salsa Dip, 38
    Breakfast Bacon Burritos, 12
    Cucumber Salsa, 37
    Pico de Gallo, 34
    Tortilla Morning, 14
Sangria, 5
sauces
    Avocado Mayonnaise, 106
    Barbecue Sauce, 98
    Chipotle Cream Sauce, 105
    Creamy Horseradish Sauce, 103
    Creole Mayonnaise, 106
    Hot Pepper Jelly Dipping Sauce, 105
    Maple-Vinegar Drizzle, 101
    Marinara Sauce, 141
    Meat Sauce for Spaghetti, 159, 160
    Perfect Hollandaise Sauce, 102
    Pizza Sauce, 107
    Remoulade Sauce, 103
    Seafood Cocktail Sauce, 104
    Tartar Sauce, 104
    Western-Style Steak Sauce, 99
    White Cream Gravy, 107
    Wine Mushroom Sauce, 101
    See also marinades

INDEX

sausages
  breakfast
    Sausage and Egg Muffins, 21
    Sausage Balls, 22
    Sausage Brunch Casserole, 13
    Southwest Egg Casserole, 16
    Tortilla Morning, 14
  chorizo
    Frijoles Rancheros Beans, 135
    Southwest Hash Browns, 25
  little smokies, 49
  Polish
    New Orleans Red Beans and Rice, 138
Sautéed Green Beans, 134
seafood
  crab
    Bourbon Street Corn and Crab Bisque, 63
    New Orleans Gumbo, 70
    Virginia Hot Crab Dip, 30
  grouper
    Grilled Grouper with Soy-Ginger Glaze, 215
  halibut
    Cornflake-Crusted Halibut with Chili-Cilantro Sauce, 212
    Oven-Fried Halibut, 210
    Pan-Seared Halibut with Bell Pepper Relish, 211
  lobster
    Grilled Lobster Tails, 201
  salmon
    Apple and Horseradish-Glazed Salmon, 205
    Grilled Bourbon-Basted Salmon, 204
    Grilled Salmon, 208
    Pan-Roasted Salmon, 207
    Salmon Patties, 209
    Salmon with Garlic Butter, 206
    sauce for, 105
  Seafood Cocktail Sauce, 104
  shrimp
    Beer Batter Fried Seafood, 201
    Bourbon Street Corn and Crab Bisque, 63
    Garlicky Grilled Shrimp, 204
    Grilled Shrimp Brochettes, 202
    New Orleans Gumbo, 70
    New Orleans-Style Barbecued Shrimp, 203
    sauces for, 104, 105
  tilapia or trout
    Blackened Tilapia, 214
    Pecan-Crusted Tilapia or Trout, 213
  tips for buying, 200
serrano chili pepper
  Cornflake-Crusted Halibut with Chili-Cilantro Sauce, 212
7 Up
  7 Up Salad, 84
  Summer Wine Cooler, 4
shallots
  Balsamic Vinaigrette, 91
  Maple Vinegar Drizzle, 101
  No-Grill Skillet Beef Tenderloin, 154
sherry, dry
  American Steakhouse-Style Beef, 153
  Show-Stopping Trifle, 285
  Stir-Fry Cashew Chicken, 182
Show Stopping Trifle, 285
shrimp
  Beer Batter Fried Seafood, 201
  Bourbon Street Corn and Crab Bisque, 63
  Garlicky Grilled Shrimp, 204
  Grilled Shrimp Brochettes, 202
  New Orleans Gumbo, 70
  New Orleans-Style Barbecued Shrimp, 203
  sauces for, 104, 105
side dishes
  brunch
    Brunch Potatoes, 25
    French Breakfast Puffs, 22
    Quick Cheese Puffs, 25
    Sausage and Egg Muffins, 21
    Sausage Balls, 22
    Southwest Hash Browns, 25
  Corn Bread Stuffing, 127
  legumes
    Baked Beans, 136
    Frijoles Rancheros Beans, 135
    New Orleans Red Beans and Rice, 138
    New Year's Southern-Style Black-Eyed Peas, 137
  pasta
    Bow Tie Pasta with Marinara Sauce, 141
    Fettuccine Alfredo, 142
    Macaroni and Cheese, 142
    New Mexico Green Chili Macaroni and Cheese, 143
    Spaghetti with Garlic, Olive Oil, and Chili Pepper, 144

rice
- Broccoli-Rice Casserole, 145
- Fried Rice, 146
- New Mexico Red Beans and Rice, 138
- Spanish Rice, 145

vegetable
- Acorn Squash, 129
- Au Gratin Potatoes, 120
- Baked Tomatoes, 133
- Broccoli-Rice Casserole, 145
- Cheddar Baked Potato Slices, 121
- Corn Soufflé, 126
- Creamed Corn, 125
- Creamed Spinach, 132
- Grandmas Lane's Fried Corn, 125
- Green Bean Casserole, 134
- Homemade Mashed Potatoes, 119
- Honey Rum Carrots, 128
- Ranch Fries, 121
- Sautéed Green Beans, 134
- Southern Comfort Sweet Potatoes, 124
- Squash Stir-Fry, 130
- Summer Squash Casserole, 131
- Sweet Potato Crunch, 123
- Twice-Baked Potatoes, 122

See also appetizers

Simple Roast Chicken, 187
sirloin steak. *See under* beef
slaws
- Grandma's Old-Fashioned Cole Slaw, 82
- Momo's Cabbage Slaw, 83
- Slow Cooker Beef Stroganoff, 155
- Slow Cooker Cherry-Cola Ham, 227

Slow Cooker Sweet and Sour Chicken, 180
Slow-Roasted Pork Tenderloin with Cranberry Sauce, 224
Smoky Marinated Beef Brisket, 153
Smothered Swiss Steak, 151
snacks. *See* appetizers
Snickerdoodle Cookies, 234

soda
cherry cola
- Slow Cooker Cherry-Cola Ham, 227

ginger ale
- Easy Shower Punch, 6
- Pink Elephant Punch, 7

7 Up
- 7 Up Salad, 84
- Easy Shower Punch, 6
- Summer Wine Cooler, 4

Sprite
- Easy Shower Punch, 6

soups
- Baked Potato Soup, 62
- Bourbon Street Corn and Crab Bisque, 63
- Chicken Tortilla Soup, 60
- Corn Chowder, 65
- Grandma Lane's Chicken and Dumplings, 67
- Mom's Chicken Soup, 68
- New Mexico Cheese and Potato Soup, 66
- New Orleans Gumbo, 70
- Pasta e Fagioli Soup (Italian Pasta and Bean Soup), 69
- Spicy Chicken Chili, 64
- Taco Soup, 59
- Texas Chili, 61

sour cream
- Buttermilk Dressing, 97

Rum Butter Sour Cream Cake, 254
Sour Cream Chicken, 169
Sour Cream Chicken Enchiladas, 177

Southern Comfort liqueur
- Southern Comfort Sweet Potatoes, 124

Southwest Avocado and Corn Dip, 32
Southwest Egg Casserole, 16
Southwest Ham and Potato Chip Skillet, 18
Southwest Hash Browns, 25

soy sauce
- American Steakhouse-Style Beef, 153
- Grilled Grouper with Soy-Ginger Glaze, 215
- No-Grill Teriyaki Chicken, 181
- Stir-Fry Cashew Chicken, 182
- Thai Chicken Salad with Peanut Dressing, 78

spaghetti
- Chicken Spaghetti, 170
- Easy Chicken with Thin Spaghetti, 196
- Oven-Baked Chili Spaghetti with Cheese, 161
- Spaghetti with Garlic, Olive Oil, and Chili Pepper, 144

Spanish Rice, 145
Spice Steak Rub, 100
Spicy Chicken Chili, 64

spinach
- Creamed Spinach, 132
- salad dressing for, 93
- Spinach Balls, 50
- Spinach Dip, 29
- Spinach Quiche, 20

INDEX

Sprite
   Summer Wine Cooler, 4
squash
   acorn, 129
   yellow
      Squash Stir-Fry, 130
      Summer Squash Casserole, 131
steak. *See under* beef
Stir-Fry Cashew Chicken, 182
stock, chicken
   Bourbon Street Corn and Crab Bisque, 63
   Texas Spicy Chicken Breasts, 179
strawberries
   chocolate dipped, 274
   Strawberry Romaine Salad, 75
Streusel Caramel Bars, 280
stuffing mix
   Spinach Balls, 50
   Swiss Cheese Chicken, 196
sugar
   Aunt Meta's Heavenly Chocolate Cake, 250
   Chocolate Brownie Cake, 247
   Dry Mix Spiced Tea, 3
   Grandma Kattner's German Apple Cake, 257
   Luscious Lemon Bars, 278
   Momo's Chocolate Sheet Cake, 249
   Potluck Pound Cake, 264
   Roll-Out Sugar Cookies for Santa, 233
   See also brown sugar; powdered sugar
Summer Squash Casserole, 131
sweet chili sauce
   Spicy Chicken Chili, 64
   Turkey Tenderloins with Sweet Chili Sauce, 198

sweetened condensed milk
   Brownie Cheesecake Bars, 276
   Chocolate Chip Cheesecake, 261
   Chocolate Peanut Butter Chip Cookies, 241
   Creamy Banana Pudding, 284
   Double Delicious Cookie Bars, 275
   Fudge Truffle Cheesecake, 262
   Key Lime Pie, 270
   Streusel Caramel Bars, 280
sweet potatoes
   Southern Comfort Sweet Potatoes, 124
   Sweet Potato Crunch, 123
Swiss cheese
   Chicken Cordon Bleu Casserole, 175
   Swiss Cheese Chicken, 196
syrup. *See* maple syrup

T

Tabasco sauce. *See* hot pepper sauce (Tabasco)
Taco Salad, 76
taco seasoning
   Mexican Layer Dip, 33
   Texas Trash Warm Bean Dip, 34
Taco Soup, 59
Tartar Sauce, 104
tea, spiced, 3
tequila
   Tequila-Glazed Grilled Chicken Breast, 183
   Tequila-Marinated Fajitas, 156
Terrific Toffee, 286
Texas Caviar, 39
Texas Chili, 61
Texas Corn Bread, 111

Texas Spicy Chicken Breasts, 179
Texas Trash Warm Bean Dip, 34
Tex-Mex dishes
   Breakfast Bacon Burritos, 12
   Chicken Tortilla Soup, 60
   Easy Beef Tacos, 162
   Easy Cheesy Beef Enchiladas, 164
   Frijoles Rancheros Beans, 135
   Mexican Layer Dip, 33
   Mexican Meat Pie, 163
   New Mexico Green Chili Macaroni and Cheese, 143
   Southwest Avocado and Corn Dip, 32
   Southwest Egg Casserole, 16
   Southwest Ham and Potato Chip Skillet, 18
   Southwest Hash Browns, 25
   Taco Salad, 76
   Taco Soup, 59
   Tequila-Marinated Fajitas, 157
   Texas Chili, 61
   Texas Corn Bread, 111
   Texas Trash Warm Bean Dip, 34
   Tortilla Morning, 14
Thai dishes
   Thai Chicken Salad with Peanut Dressing, 78
Thanksgiving dishes
   Roast Turkey, 197
tilapia
   Blackened Tilapia, 214
   Pecan-Crusted Tilapia or Trout, 213
toffee, 286
tomatoes
   beefsteak
      Baked Tomatoes, 133
      Momo's Cucumber Salad, 83

    Primavera Salad, 81
cherry
    Baja Pork Stir-Fry, 220
chopped
    American Chop Suey, 165
    Bow Tie Pasta with Marinara Sauce, 141
    New Orleans Gumbo, 70
    Spanish Rice, 145
    East Texas Baked Tomatoes, 133
    Momo's Cucumber Salad, 83
grape
    Garden Salad with Ranchy Vinaigrette, 74
juice
    Oven-Baked Chili Spaghetti with Cheese, 161
paste
    Pizza Sauce, 107
peeled
    Black Bean Salsa Dip, 38
    Mexican Layer Dip, 33
    Momma's Meatloaf, 149
    Pico de Gallo, 34
    Southwest Avocado and Corn Dip, 32
    Taco Soup, 59
whole
    Chicken Cacciatore, 171
    Frijoles Rancheros Beans, 135
    Meat Sauce for Spaghetti, 159
    Mexican Meat Pie, 163
    Oven-Baked Chili Spaghetti with Cheese, 161
    See also Rotel diced tomatoes and green chilies
tortillas
    Breakfast Bacon Burritos with, 12
    Chicken Tortilla Soup, 60
    Easy Cheesy Beef Enchiladas, 164
    Mexican Meat Pie, 163
    New Mexico Cheese and Potato Soup, 66
    Sour Cream Chicken Enchiladas, 177
    Tortilla Morning, 14
    Tortilla Roll-Ups, 47
Traditional Toll House Cookies, 240
trifle, 285
trout
    Pecan-Crusted Tilapia or Trout, 213
tuna, white albacore
    Tuna Salad, 78
turkey
    gravy for, 108
    Primavera Salad, 81
    Roast Turkey, 197
    Turkey Tenderloins with Sweet Chili Sauce, 198
Turtle Brownies, 281
Twice-Baked Potatoes, 122

U

unsweetened cocoa. *See under* chocolate

V

vanilla wafers
    Creamy Banana Pudding, 284
    Fudge Truffle Cheesecake, 262
veal, sauces for, 101
Velveeta cheese
    Chicken Spaghetti, 170
    Chili Cheese Dip, 35
    Easy Cheesy Beef Enchiladas, 164
    Macaroni and Cheese, 142
    Mexican Meat Pie, 163
vermouth, dry
    Slow Cooker Beef Stroganoff, 155
vinaigrettes
    Balsamic Vinaigrette, 91
    Garden Salad with Ranchy Vinaigrette, 74
    Vinaigrette, 91
vinegar. *See specific types*
Virginia Hot Crab Dip, 30
vodka
    Pink Elephant Punch, 7

W

wafers, vanilla
    Creamy Banana Pudding, 284
    Fudge Truffle Cheesecake, 262
waffles, 11
Warm Honey Dijon Chicken Salad, 77
water chestnuts
    Classic Chicken Ring, 172
    Spinach Dip, 29
watermelon
    Fruit Salad, 86
Wedge salad dressings, 94, 95
Weiderstein Applesauce Cake, 256
Weiderstein Chocolate Cookies, 239
Western-Style Steak Sauce, 99
whipping cream
    Aunt Meta's Heavenly Holiday Salad, 84
    Millionaire Mousse Cake, 248
whiskey
    Bourbon Pecan Pie, 269
    Grilled Bourbon-Basted Salmon, 204
    Pan-Roasted Salmon, 207

Pork Chops with Bourbon-
    Glazed Onions, 225
white chocolate
    Millionaire Mousse Cake, 248
White Cream Gravy, 107
white wine
    Lemon Chicken Picatta, 184
    River Road Oven Chicken, 192
    Salmon with Garlic Butter, 206
    Slow Cooker Beef Stroganoff, 155
    Texas Spicy Chicken Breasts, 179
white wine vinegar
    Caesar Salad, 73
    Garden Salad with Ranchy Vinaigrette, 74
    Old-Fashioned German Potato Salad, 80
    Primavera Salad, 81
    Roquefort Dressing, 95
Wild Turkey bourbon whiskey, 204
wine
    Chicken Picatta with Marsala Sauce, 185
    Lemon Chicken Picatta, 184
    Sangria, 5
    Summer Wine Cooler, 4
    tip for, 2
    Virginia Hot Crab Dip, 30
    Western-Style Steak Sauce, 99
    Wine Mushroom Sauce, 101
    See also white wine
Worcestershire sauce
    Amber's Texas-Style Steak Marinade, 99
    Barbecue Sauce, 98
    Holiday Meatballs, 44
    Italian Meatballs, 158
    Momma's Meatloaf, 149

Mushroom Pork Chops, 221
New Orleans-Style Barbecued Shrimp, 203
Patty's Party Mix, 54
Russian Dressing, 92
Salmon Patties, 209
Smoky Marinated Beef Brisket, 153
Smothered Swiss Steak, 151
Western-Style Steak Sauce, 99

Z

zucchini
    Squash Stir-Fry, 130
    Summer Squash Casserole, 131
    Zucchini Bread, 114
    Zucchini Carrot Cake, 258

About the Author

Patty Hensel has a passion for cooking and a love for entertaining guests. She is a native Texan, born in New Braunfels, and has been married to her husband Steve for over thirty-two years. They have two beautiful daughters and raised them in the same house for over twenty-five years. She understands deeply how hearth and home can define a family, as all of her childhood and motherhood memories started in the kitchen.